Experts Wisdom

Life-Changing Principles and Transformational Business Strategies from the Go-To Authorities

Debbie Allen

Best Selling Author of
The Highly Paid Expert

A Collection of Wisdom
From World Class Experts

AUTHENTIC ENDEAVORS
PUBLISHING
www.AuthenticEndeavorsPublishing.com

Authentic Endeavors Publishing
AuthenticEndeavorsPublishing.com

©2015 Authentic Endeavors Inc,
All rights reserved.
No part of this book may be reproduced by mechanical,
photographic, or electronic process, or in the form of recording, nor
may it be stored in a retrieval system, transmitted or otherwise be
copied for public use or private use – other than "fair use" as brief
quotations embodied in articles and reviews, without prior written
permission of the publisher and/or authors.

This book is designed to provide information and inspiration to our
readers. It is sold with the understanding that the publisher and
the authors are not engaged in the rendering of psychological, legal,
accounting or other professional advice. The content is the sole
expression and opinion of the authors and not necessarily of the
publisher. No warranties or guaranties are expressed or implied by
the publisher's choice to include any of the content in this book.
Neither the publisher nor the authors shall be liable for any
physical, psychological, emotional, financial, or commercial
damages, including but not limited to special, incidental,
consequential or other damages. Our views and rights are the
same: You are responsible for your own choices, actions and
results.

Published by Authentic Endeavors Publishing
www.AuthenticEndeavors.com

ISBN: 978-0692522646

Dedication

Debbie Allen

This insightful book is dedicated to some of my amazing mentors and expert students who have chosen to create a ripple effect on the world with their passion, skills, talent and knowledge.

These hand-selected experts choose to make a difference in the lives of others every day. To do this they had to first make a decision to claim the title of 'expert' and truly become the go-to authority in their niche market.

A high level of responsibility goes along with claiming this level of expertise. It's about developing a business that is larger than oneself. An expert builds a business that holds the responsibility for continuous life-long learning and to give back to others as a global leader.

I honor the experts in this book who have chosen to come together in a collaborative effort to create an impactful book of collective wisdom. They openly share their stories, expertise and gifts with you.

i

Introduction to Experts Wisdom

Debbie Allen

This book came together with the collaborative efforts of many high-level experts. Some include my own mentors whose wisdom I wanted to share with you. Other experts in this book include some of my amazing clients who have studied under me to position their business for expert success. These students made a commitment to be the very best at what they do.

An expert is someone who is widely recognized as a reliable source for a specific skill, passion or body of knowledge far beyond the average person. An expert has extensive knowledge and experience in a particular area. Experts are called upon for their advice and *wisdom* on their respective subject.

Some of the experts in this book have impressive credentials, advanced training and education while others simply have experienced business and life first hand as entrepreneurs growing, building and selling companies.

This I know for sure... one thing all of the experts in this book have in common is the fact that they are all wise individuals who have worked hard to be recognized for their *wisdom* and sound judgment.

There are many books available that offer a wide array of authors. What makes this book unique is that the stories are shared by the 'true' experts from diverse industries who have 'been there and done that'. They had the same goal in mind; to give you solid ideas, solutions and results in every area of your life and business.

As you read each chapter some stories will speak directly to you as if they were written just for you. Other ideas shared may bring you straightforward advice, inspiration and even powerful motivation to help you step up to becoming an expert yourself.

This book was designed to give you bite-sized bits of information from a variety of viewpoints so that you can then brainstorm your own life's direction and implement the strategies you need. You'll come up with new ideas simply by taking a walk in another's shoes through the pages of this book. Each expert offers steps for you to take so you can grow change and expand your success faster.

Thank you for investing in this book and making a commitment to learn from the wisdom of others.

Enjoy the read!

Debbie

Table of Contents

The Shift to Making a Difference

Debbie Allen

Succeeding in new things creates confidence.
Confidence in turn creates unstoppable success.

As an entrepreneur, my background in business started at a very young age, but I had no formal business training except for what I learned from the school of hard knocks. I've built and sold numerous million dollar companies and although I've had many successes in my life, there came a time where I felt something was missing. That "something" was giving back to others. I had been blessed with having the opportunity to work with many wonderful mentors and experts throughout my life and believed it was time for me to begin supporting others with the *wisdom* I had learned while growing and marketing my own businesses. Yet, I had no idea how to go about becoming an expert myself.

Make the shift to becoming more fulfilled.

It's making the shift in belief from "How can I

make more money?" to "What can I do to serve others?" that has made a difference in my own life and the lives of many students around the world. When you let go of simply chasing the next dollar and focus on how to best share your gifts, talents and *wisdom* with the world, you begin to develop a business around your passion. I discovered that when you feed both your passion and wisdom, powerful opportunities begin to flow to you as if you are a magnet.

After I made this shift it not only fulfilled my heart, it also filled up my bank account. I was making more money than I could ever imagine.

You've heard the saying, "Do what you love, and the money will follow."

Is this actually true? If you follow your passion and pursue what you love doing for a living, will the monetary rewards really follow? What I've discovered is that having passion certainly helps - but you'll need more than that to grow a lucrative career as an expert that supports others in return. Having passion will give you the drive and determination you'll need when the road gets rocky or times get challenging. Skills and talent are required to make a name for yourself; but passion, skills and talent alone won't pay the bills.

We all have a life journey, a story, a message, or skill that will help and inspire others. What matters most is how we share our message. We are all were born into this world to make a difference by giving back to others in some way. When you share your advice and *wisdom* with the world, you begin to receive the most amazing gifts in return; including a more fulfilled and abundantly free lifestyle.

You'll know when this commitment of giving back feels right because you will truly be living and breathing your own legacy ... Yes, LIVING your legacy ... not just leaving it behind when you exit the planet.

If you have ever been mentored, guided or coached by someone in any way; you understand the feeling of being supported by someone who believes in you. Maybe they even believed in you more than you believed in yourself at that time. This may have caused a shift in you too. Your beliefs were shifted and changed forever, making you a better person in some way.

A shift, no matter how small, can be a life-changing experience.

When you've been supported, it makes you want to support others in having the same type of shift. Imagine a life of giving back by lifting others up in the form of inspiration, motivation, knowledge and commitment to do better; shifting them to a better life in some way. Imagine being able to support others in this same magical way while passing on your own experiences.

3

Every positive shift in someone's life holds energy. This same energy continues to grow and consistently expands. When you help others do better and to believe in themselves, everyone around them does better too. That's truly your gift of *wisdom* having a ripple effect!

Your wisdom, skills, talents, vision and enthusiasm to support others is priceless. No one can view the world exactly like you. No other person on this earth has the same experiences, personal values and viewpoints as you do. You have the ability to put our own fingerprint on the world and make a difference now.

Shifting requires you to ignore conventional approaches and pave your own path.

If you want to stand out in this world, you must get really serious about doing something different and moving away from the 'sea of sameness.' Focus on being different.

Ordinarily, we achieve conventional *wisdom* following conventional ideas. We experience reasonable gains when we rely on reasonable approaches. You may find ways to make modest improvements and in turn, make a modest income. But, if you go looking for nothing more than that, you will only have modest gains.

Experts stand out and get noticed for the

differences they make, not by following the status quo. They create quantum leaps by abandoning what's been done and said before. Instead of once again doing what you have always done, shift to an even more powerful intensity and determination to be different.

A shift like this requires an abrupt change in behavior. You must do something new and different!

The tendency, when you begin to stall out or get stuck when starting out, is to go back to the basics and do what you do "best." But doing what you do best can be the worst thing you can do. It really doesn't matter how well you can do something if it's the wrong thing for you to do.

For example, my brother Terry is a highly successful entrepreneur who's built his own million dollar business. He's been an entrepreneur from a very young age, just like me. We both grew up in a family car rental business as teenagers, learning the business as we grew it step-by-step. When Terry was in his late twenties he left the business for about a year to pursue a career he was much more passionate about.

When he left, it gave me the courage and commitment to pursue my own passion. So I left the family business too, to start a business on my own that I was more passionate about. I've never looked back since that day and believe me when I say, "If I'm not having fun, I'm not going to do it anymore."

But after about a year, my brother went back to the car rental business and purchased it from my father. He has been running that same business now for over forty years. It's a very successful business, but he hates it and can't wait to get out and sell it. HATE is a strong word. I'm sure he enjoys the income and security but he feels trapped because he's bored and not fulfilling his passion. He's just making money but he is not feeling fulfilled. There's nothing wrong with making lots of money, I'm all for that, but why settle for just money when you can LOVE what you do and make even more money in return?

If you don't shift to shaking things up, years can go by like they did for my brother. You can find yourself doing the same thing for far too long.

Faith in the familiar can keep you stuck and unhappy in your career.

Shifting may require an abrupt change in your direction and behaviors. To thrive in life, you must do something new, something inspiring that keeps you excited every day; something that drives you to succeed despite any obstacle.

You shift when you reinvent yourself and your business. This requires you to break out of the rut or routine you've been hanging on to.

Start by second-guessing your daily routines and overcome the addiction to your own methodologies. Set a new pattern, a new intention; one you are excited and passionate about - one that utilizes your *wisdom* and supports others in return.

If the things you're doing bore you or are no longer working, stop doing them. Focus on what works. If you'll just quit what you've been doing and allow some 'space', new opportunities will instantly appear.

Create a bigger vision.

The majority of people can be found flying too close to the ground. Too often they don't give themselves permission to soar.

Get uncomfortable. Prepare yourself for "Mr. Toad's Wild Ride." You're going to cover some unfamiliar territory and encounter obstacles you've never faced before. It can feel like a roller coaster out of control when the safety of your behavior patterns is being stretched to the limit. The normal reaction is to want to hold on tight. But you're going to have to learn to let go if you truly want to soar.

If you feel uncomfortable, that's a good sign. If you are experiencing no anxiety or discomfort, the risk you're taking probably isn't worth it for you. The only risks that aren't a little scary are the ones you've outgrown. A high comfort level provides solid evidence that you're 'playing it safe' not growing, not really testing your limits at all and not in the process of a major shift. You might be making gradual progress, but you're clearly not going for a breakthrough.

If you focus on the possibilities, rather than obstacles, quantum shifts become possible. This requires moving outside of your mental boundaries. If you learn how to rethink the way you are currently thinking - you will expand and multiply your potential. Allow yourself to be guided instead of staying stuck.

You don't have to know how you're going to get there, but you need to know where you want to go. It is critical to have a crystal clear picture of what you want to accomplish. A sharply defined mental vision of your outcome will clear the path for you to get there faster. Commitment and determination will allow you to "keep away the squirrels" and remain focused on your goal.

Where do you want to be in one year from now - what does your business and your life look like?

Visualize your arrival!

When you visualize, it's like you "magnetize

and move" yourself to the ways and means involved in getting there. Solutions begin to appear and answers come to you much easier. But you must be able to tolerate obstacles, confusion and even a bit of chaos as you shift. Don't hold on to problems or challenges along the way. Move past roadblocks, stay committed to your passion and enjoy the journey.

You'll make some mistakes along the way but those "mistakes" are simply required lessons in the process of making a profound shift. Keep in mind that your "mistakes" must be profound enough to be able to share and create an impact on the lives of others. They are your lessons to learn and share with the world.

You can't hold up in a safe zone of behavior where you have beaten the odds of failing.

You must be willing to encounter defeat and open to running into problems or you will never have the opportunity to test the limits of what you truly are capable of accomplishing. Again, if you are experiencing no difficulties, problems or pain, you have probably aimed too low. You've leveled off in your growth and achievement. You are limiting your potential. Think of your "mistakes" as a positive sign - lessons in disguise. They are simply a temporary loss of momentum that occurs in the process of shifting gears.

Failure doesn't mean you are defeated; struggle actually gives you strength! Don't interpret problems as proof that you should quit or stay stuck. Take them as evidence of your growth and improvement instead.

Forget the idea that you should be able to see tangibly and in full view, all of the resources necessary to leverage your shift dramatically. You can't achieve your full potential though your own singular struggle or shift. Don't do it all alone. Your own power is actually based upon the support of others - other experts. You will begin to pay attention to others ideas when you need them. When they appear, be open and coachable. These unforeseen resources can make amazing contributions in your efforts.

Often, resources and opportunities come to you as unseen forces through your subconscious mind, intuition and even luck. Inspiration can appear at any time. A creative solution to a problem may come to you from this book. A breakthrough idea can flash through your mind at any time. Somehow the resources and opportunities you need will just seem to appear by coincidence. When this happens, paint a picture in your mind so that you become even clearer on what you want and how you'll make an impact.

Shifts come easy when you plug into these

remarkable resources. When you focus constantly on a clear picture of what you want to accomplish and move toward it confidently, the unseen forces will rally to your support.

Shifts happen when you seek a solution that serves both yourself and others. Overall, it requires less energies and emotions and becomes less demanding. Yet shifting requires you to violate the boundary of the probable. It means achieving well beyond the obvious or the conventional.

Don't limit yourself to what you have - start going after what you want.

This means giving yourself permission to take risks. This is the only way you can set your intention to live a passionate, independent, financially free lifestyle. You only have one life to live!

Instead of holding back because you don't know the 'how'... just make the jump. Act as if your success is already guaranteed. Act in spite of fear, doubt or worry.

What's holding you back from the shift you deserve?

Your mindset, for the moment, may be blinded

by doubt or skepticism. The idea of making a shift in your business, jumping from the present level of achievement to one several stages higher is one bold move. It may feel a bit far-fetched to you now, but that may only be because you haven't been trained to think that way. You may currently believe that you can't make much improvement at all... much less a quantum shift. Sadly, most people only achieve about ten percent of their true potential.

False beliefs are easy to carry around in your mind and are self-imposed limitations. Beliefs can put a ceiling on how far you reach and fly. Your real limits are far beyond your mental boundaries.

If you have doubts they are not the product of accurate thinking and beliefs, they are simply your habitual thinking. Something may have happened in your past that makes you hold on to this false belief. This may also cause you to take fewer risks.

People who take risks create bold experiences that cause them to create impactful breakthroughs in their lives.

If you feel it's time for you to make a bold move and/or find a new path, this book will speak to you with many voices. Listen to the stories of those who were bold enough to change and make a dramatic shift in their own lives.

Put away any limiting beliefs and ideas and start going for it! What you want becomes the driving force that shifts you to action.

Place your trust in action! Living a life of passion means you must leave your comfort zone (your safety net) behind. It only keeps you from growing and expanding.

The way to move past 'limiters' is to give up some of your old beliefs, patterns and ideas by sacrificing some 'safe' and 'sensible' thinking patterns. Become open to new ideas, new ways of doing things - think and act way outside of the box.

Passion fires your soul and fills your spirit. It energizes your heart and mind, allowing you to perform at much higher levels of success.

Allow your passion to ignite your determination to achieve more.

Passion must be filed with visions of a dream that are dramatic enough to make a big difference. Your emotional intensity must burn hot enough to protect you against the chilling effects of doubt, uncertainty, criticism and failure. Only deep desire can generate such heat.

For example, when I'm speaking to an audience, my natural enthusiasm for what I teach allows energy to flow into me like a flame. Since I've learned to speak my mind and share my own one true voice, my natural passion shines through every time. It's never forced because it's authentically me. This fire never lets me down because every word I speak comes from soul and my spirit, a place that resides both inside my heart and my head.

For you to care this intensely there must be something worth caring about, something remarkable, special, unique and big enough to light the fire in your heart.

The only way to do this is to loosen the limits of your thinking, and give yourself permission to speak your mind and become your true self. Your inner drive must be strong enough to carry you past the point of worrying about what others think if you truly want to make an impact.

Remember, you are not going for status quo here, you are a difference maker and difference makers need to rock the boat a bit.

The world is looking for you. Others need your advice, guidance, spunk, guts, confidence and courage along with your *wisdom*. They are looking at you as their thought leader to follow.

Stepping up to a bigger game in business and in life means stepping up to 'owning' your passion by becoming the expert at what you know and love as you support others with your *wisdom* and experiences.

There is no better time to launch yourself as an

expert than right now! Everyone is looking for experts online. The Internet has brought the world to our doorstep.

You have an 'expert' inside of you just waiting to get out and step up to a bigger game. There is so much more for you to achieve! What lies within your reach will astound you. When you step up and make that shift, the world will take notice and be there waiting to hear your words.

Debbie Allen is an internationally recognized business and brand strategist and is also known as "The Expert of Experts." She is the bestselling author of 7 books including *The Highly Paid Expert* and *Experts Wisdom.*

Debbie has presented before thousands in 28 countries and is ranked as one of the top professional women speakers worldwide. She is an award winning entrepreneur who has built and sold six million-dollar companies. Today, she supports clients in positioning themselves as the go-to expert in their niche market to stand out and dominate over their competition. Debbie mentors small business owners, entrepreneurs, coaches, speakers and experts in diverse industries.

Learn more about Debbie's extensive expertise, live events and personalized mentoring programs at www.DebbieAllen.com.

The majority of people can be found flying too close to the ground. Too often they don't give themselves permission to soar.
~ Debbie Allen

Become an Inspired Leader

Carolyn Andrews

When you share your vision and passion with others you will achieve success together.

Inspired...it seems to be a "buzz" word these days. Do we even know what it means? Inspired is defined as:

"Of extraordinary quality, as if arising from some external creative impulse."

"Of such surpassing brilliance or excellence as to suggest divine inspiration."

We know inspiring others is important, so who should I inspire and why? I believe the answer will take your life, career and achievements to the next level. To truly achieve success, the key is to be inspired and to be able to inspire those around you.

You can't share what you don't already have so before you can inspire others, you have to create your own inspiration. The first step for me was to understand my "Why;" my purpose in life.

Simon Sinek, in his book, *Start with Why,* asks, *"Do you know your why; the purpose, cause or belief that inspires you to do what you do?"* His book is a great resource to help you uncover your why and begin the journey to inspiration.

It all starts with you! Ask yourself what you want in business and in life. Do you have a clear understanding of where you want to go? Part of the process is discovering what it is that you truly want and believe you deserve. Once you know, it's time to uncover what is stopping you from getting what you really want.

Becoming an Inspired Leader starts with BEING INSPIRED yourself.

Take a moment and ask yourself these questions:

"What is it that makes my heart and soul sing?"

"If I could spend my day doing something I absolutely love that would have a ripple effect out into the world what would that be?"

Find something special that makes your eyes light up when you think about it and makes you glow when you talk about it. It's something that will create a greater good for everyone around you, whether that's business, community or family.

Inspiration is something that penetrates all aspects of our life. For now, let's focus on business even though the principles apply equally to family and community.

How do you want to touch lives each day? How

do you want to be remembered?

It doesn't matter what your job title is, you can take an appropriate leadership role within your business responsibilities and develop a clear vision of where you are going. Clarity and passion are keys to influencing those around you to get excited and stay motivated about the goals you all want to achieve. When we have successes and recognize and celebrate them, it encourages everyone to continue striving for greater success. As we grow and develop our new skills, we build confidence which leads us to be productive and happy. As inspiration grows, it ripples out to others.

Your passion and success, coupled with your inspired leadership and guidance will change lives. You know what's possible but you might not be there yet. You might have times when you go through the day stressed, disengaged and unfulfilled, let's change that! You might be a business owner who says "this is not why I started a business; I am working harder than before, with financial risks and too much stress." Maybe you are a corporate employee who leaves exhausted at the end of each day and wonders how long you can keep up the routine of feeling completely unfulfilled and are dreading going to work every morning. You might ask "is this all there is?" Are you someone who is doing their best to "survive until retirement waiting to do the things you have always dreamed of?"

The good news is that changing those feelings by finding inspiration and success usually does not require you to find a new job or start a new business. You can be happy where you are just by redefining what you do and why you do it. To over simplify it, inspiration will come when you look at your work from a new perspective. Sometimes though, finding it turns your world upside down; so be ready for whatever comes your way!

When I was a computer professional, I loved creating programs that would automate processes and make life easier. It was challenging with obvious and immediate results. I had a great feeling of accomplishment as I was able to see the progress immediately. When I stepped into a leadership role, much of that tangible reward disappeared. I realized that I didn't look forward to going to work anymore, in fact I dreaded it. Did I need to change jobs or go to a different company? I didn't want to! I admired my company and really cared about and respected the people I worked with. The thought of leaving and starting over was terrifying to me.

When I shared my discontent with one of my mentors, he asked me if I knew my "why." Of course there are the standard answers...I work for the money and because it is expected of me. I realized that wasn't what he meant...so I told him that helping others was important to me. I helped others when there was an assignment or task to be done. I just never thought about taking actions that made life better for others. That's what my community volunteer efforts were for. The reality is opportunities surround us all the time. I asked myself questions like, "What is important to me?" and "How do I think I can make a difference in the world through my work?" What if I understood my purpose? Could I find a way to incorporate that into my job and would it help me to achieve to the best of my ability and even find joy? The answer is definitely YES!

I realized that my purpose was to help others to reach great heights of performance and success and be proud of their accomplishments while enjoying each day. To share that, I had to be living it. I discovered that my management role wasn't to *tell* people what to do or what was wrong; my role was to encourage them to identify and develop their strengths and create an environment where they could contribute and feel successful. I didn't need to motivate them, I needed to inspire them. When they were in the right roles, using their individual skills and talents to create results, they were *always* engaged and motivated.

I wasn't there to manage people; I was there to create an inspired environment that would allow them to be the best they could be while making a difference for themselves and in the lives of our customers. With that revelation, I created a vision of a different work space where we would grow and learn while achieving great results while having fun; a place where we could accomplish more than we thought possible. I shared my passion and vision with my team and we were able see the joy we would have in achieving success together. I had to learn how to use my own skills and strengths in new ways to inspire others to work at their highest level and enjoy what they were doing. I didn't need to find a new job; I needed to find my own inspiration.

When I left the corporate world and started my coaching business, I asked those same questions again. I used the understanding of my "why" to create a new vision. I knew that helping business owners understand their purpose and passion to create their vision would help them avoid hardships and have the rewards they deserved. Not only would they achieve success financially and personally, they would improve the lives of their employees and their families.

Each corporate leader who I helped to learn and practice inspiration could inspire their team members and have a positive effect on the each employee and increase the success of the company.

Very soon I realized that through inspiration and empowerment many people would grow and prosper; lives would change and businesses would flourish. At the same time I was helping one person, they were helping many others. Why would I stop there? Could it be possible that this would be the way for me to leave a legacy? YES, because my "why" and my purpose in life is to help others. I had to step it up to a bigger game. I wanted to make a greater difference! That is when I realized that becoming an expert in Inspired Leadership was the key for me.

It is for you, too. So, I will ask the question again... what is your "why?" Use it to find your inspiration and you will be on your way to inspiring others! I promise you, life will never be the same!

So how do you make it happen? Inspired Leaders lead by example. Here is my 3 step formula for being an Inspired Leader.

EXCEL * ACHIEVE * INSPIRE

EXCEL in all that you do by learning, growing and developing the skills that you need to succeed. Practice what you have learned until you become proficient and then keep getting better. Remember, this is part of what you are purposed to do. Creating a clear vision and mission is just the beginning. Define values that will help you succeed and will keep you in alignment with your vision, insuring you will stay on the right path.

Now you're ready to **ACHIEVE**! Take it to the next level. Create goals that will make the vision your daily reality. Make them actionable and visualize yourself achieving them. Be clear about what you want and be the best you can be at whatever you do.

Learn all you can in your field of expertise. Read and glean knowledge from the experience of others. Find out who is doing what you want to be doing. Ask them how they got to be an expert. Adopt the methods they used, and practice, practice, practice.

Stay inspired and **INSPIRE** others. Bring your vision, passion and knowledge together to drive results. Actions speak loudly; who you are and how you show up daily is as important as what you say. This is where your values and beliefs take center stage in all you do.

You inspire others when they trust you and believe in the vision you are sharing. Your passion and enthusiasm will be contagious and create a ripple effect touching those around you, ultimately helping them create their own journey of believing, learning and collaborating. People need to feel included, not just in the outcome, but all along the way. We all relate well to stories; they are a great way to bring others into the journey to inspired success. Remember to tell your story in a way that your listeners feel a part of where you are going, they relate to and are included as part of the journey and the outcome.

To keep the engagement going, create conversations about what the outcomes will mean to them – more opportunity for growth, job security, learning, better compensation. Show them what is possible and what is in it for them.

A key success strategy is *Empowerment.* That means taking risks and trusting people (and yourself) to find new ways to do things, new products to develop and new processes to improve speed and profits. Lead with guidance not interference...and no taking over if it isn't the way you would do it. You might find out that their way is better than yours.

Here are some other Empowerment strategies:

- Learn how to teach others what they need to know with support and encouragement.

- Delegate appropriately and allow others to take on responsibility.

- Develop controls (goals, targets, deadlines) and monitor progress.

- Feel confident managing the risk of empowerment knowing that failure is a possibility.

- Understand the value of coaching. Encourage everyone to be better. Praise them when they succeed!

Becoming a truly inspiring leader is not about how great *you* are, it is about your ability to recognize strengths, talent and potential in others. It is the result of your own internal inspiration and your ability to communicate a vision clearly and persuasively. It happens because you believe in a cause bigger than yourself. You bring out the best in everyone around you and you effectively and passionately Excel, Achieve and Inspire!

Carolyn Andrews is a certified business and executive coach, international speaker and consultant who utilizes her experience from 30 years of corporate leadership and the development of multiple small businesses to guide individuals to excel in leadership, achieve results and become inspired leaders.

An Inspired Leader is someone who recognizes, appreciates and develops leadership in every person within an organization. They believe that everyone should work to their strengths and achieve success personally and professionally while building a positive and productive environment.

Carolyn will work with you to develop a collaborative environment that has a strong culture of communication, high-performance and increased synergy. She will guide you to achieve your true potential and teach you to inspire others.

Take the first step – Go to InspiredLeadersNow.com to receive your free e-book, *7 Steps to Becoming an Inspired Leader.*

Are you ready to **Excel**, **Achieve** and **Inspire**? Connect with Carolyn at Carolyn@InspiredLeadersNow.com

It Just Takes a Little Heart and Soul

Barbara Yager

Heart and soul are the wings of a business.
When you get it right, your business will soar.

There were six people sitting around the conference room table, three from my team and three from my prospective business partner's team. Negotiating contracts always held a certain thrill for me. I view contracts as a puzzle; you need to get all the pieces in the correct place if you expect to get the picture right.

That particular morning, the negotiations were proving to be very slow and difficult, but not more so than the many other times I found myself in the same rough waters. Explaining our position on liability, on a particularly difficult provision, was not getting the other side to move toward sharing the liabilities if there was a breakdown in their processes.

My career as a corporate legal advisor was a dream career. It was fast paced, complex and thrilling. It suited every aspect of my mercurial

31

personality. But on that day, for some unwelcome reason, the process felt dreary and uncomfortable. I could not put my finger on the source of my discomfort. Returning to the negotiation table after a brief break, I once again addressed the pivotal position from a different perspective. With patience and precision, I proposed alternative language and the reason we needed the change. Finally, there was a breakthrough and we arrived at a successful conclusion to the negotiations. With the customary handshakes and pleasantries, we bid our newest business partners farewell.

Returning to my office, I sat down at my desk and looked at the mountain of work staring at me. Normally I would just take it in stride, but not that day. I distinctly remember turning my chair toward the window as I looked out into the foggy morning. While watching the sun burn the fog away, the realization of my discomfort hit me like a lightning bolt. I was done with this career! After 22 years of running legal interference for a six-billion-dollar company, I had hit the wall and knew it was time to move on.

The time had finally arrived. I wanted to embark on a new career path that involved doing what I truly loved. I wanted to reinvent myself as a professional speaker and business coach. The thought of following my dream sent a chill of excitement through my body.

How did I know this was my direction? During my corporate career, I had the privilege of speaking to each incoming new employee group. Every six weeks, for over ten years, I had two hours to share stories with them that included a very important message. I explained that, success and growth into happy employees who loved their jobs and the company they worked for depended on one thing...their attitude. I told them that happy employees are careful employees who follow the rules that are in place to protect their company.

I shared what life was like in the corporation and how we had to work together to protect the organization. They became my "converts" and learned to care for and protect our organization as part of my "liability adverse army."

My ability to connect with them and instill a sense of personal confidence for success gave me tremendous satisfaction. I also got many comments, emails and thank-you notes which included a similar sentiment–that I should consider a career as a motivational speaker. Their accolades started to ring true with me and in secret moments, I dreamed of taking the podium and sharing the wisdom of business and life with others. That became my favorite daydream.

It took two years to wind my legal career down so when I left there would not be a gaping hole.

You see, not only was I a legal advisor but also a mentor, teacher and visionary for many people. I helped to manage risk at many levels and my vision for success was shared with my teams.

On my last day of work, in mid-August of 2012, I walked out the door and away from my career and on that same day, at that very moment, my journey as an expert began. While I knew I wanted to speak to inspire others, I had no idea what I wanted speak about. Many people who make a living in the experts' industry know with great clarity, when they start, what their expertise will be.

Nope, not me. I felt that I had so much to share, but what were my passion and direction? Just like in contract negotiations, I felt it was not prudent to rush the process. So I took some time off and just hung out. I traveled, visited with my sisters and got married to the love of my life, Steve. Cupid's arrow strikes at any age. I enjoyed just being Barb. I needed time to take the "lawyer shoes" off and put them away. It was frightening as I look back, because those were the only shoes I knew and the only ones I felt comfortable in. My new "speaker/expert" shoes felt very uncomfortable, like I was wearing six-inch heels and trying to run in them.

When someone would inquire as to my line of work, I would reply, "I am a motivational speaker."

But each time the words felt strange and uncomfortable as I replied.

To gain clarity and focus, I studied up on the speaking profession and joined my local National Speakers Association Chapter. I met many speakers and when visiting their websites I could clearly see their defined niches. Seeing site after site, I wondered how and when I would find my clarity of purpose. What should my niche be? Because of my diverse business background, the possibilities for subject matter expertise were quite broad.

After a great deal of thought, I decided to abandon the traditional wisdom of having a single, clearly defined niche and instead, I built an umbrella niche. I became the "Happiness at Work Expert." Under this niche I could talk about happiness, employee engagement, effective communication and organizational culture. Finally, the girl without a niche arrived with an umbrella. The dots got connected and I started to feel comfortable in my new shoes in ways I had not previously felt. I also felt that with a few more strides I actually might be able to break these new shoes in nicely.

Even though I was standing in the middle of the highly robust experts' industry, I still felt like I was on the outside looking in without actually *being* in the circle myself. Why? I knew I had all the right determination, education, expertise, experience and focus.

Coming out of a dream early one morning, I heard the message loud and clear. The words were, "Bring your heart and soul." My heart and soul? What did that mean? Suddenly, the realization hit me. While I built my business based on my intellectual know how, an essential piece of the puzzle was missing.

I realized that without adding my heart and soul into the process of turning expert, I would not truly believe in my work or feel my worth. At that point I started to let my internal voices speak louder than my highly developed logical and legal mind. Once I completed my website, logo, business cards and other core details, I refocused my efforts.

The process of sitting down to write a blog or create a new product offering took on a whole new focus. Instead of leading with logic, I led with feeling. What I was *feeling* became more important than what I was *thinking.* Magically, a whole new way of doing business opened up to me.

I started attracting business partners who were focused on heart-centered business and customer (or client) solutions. I spent years and years in my career as an attorney focused only on the logical side of business. It's no wonder joining the experts' industry felt so foreign to me in the beginning. I soon learned from conscious, spiritual experts that when you add heart and soul to any business it all but ensures your success. The old adage, *do what you love and the money will follow*, is true as long as there is heart and soul involved.

Suddenly, the shoes that felt previously so uncomfortable started to fit like they were custom made for me. My presentations grew in depth and meaning. I was more readily able to connect with my audiences, and business consulting took on a whole new and meaningful focus. I found that leading with heart provided more satisfying and robust solutions for my clients.

My business relationships deepened as I formed true and satisfying partnerships with my clients. Gone were my doubts and feeling of being on the outside looking in. I had finally claimed my place as an expert!

Looking back on the process, I call myself the "backwards and blind" expert. I backed into my niche with blinders on. No matter. I got to where I needed to go.

What has the process of turning expert taught me? Let me share with you three of my most powerful strategies:

- Take the first step toward your dream. Over thinking and over analyzing can cause paralysis that may keep you from your dream. Don't wait for the perfect time or topic to hit you before getting started. Perfection is a killer of creativity and motivation. Just pick something you want to focus on and get started. The rest will work itself out.

- While you are thinking through things... feel through things, too. Those feelings are signals to pay attention. Gut feelings trump logic when it comes to becoming an authentic expert. If you are having trouble balancing the scale between logic and feeling, consult with a conscious spiritual business expert.

- Beware of getting lost in the sea of advice out in the world. So many people will offer their unsolicited advice. You have to be very clear (and here is where listening to your gut is so important) about who you are at the soul level and where you want to head with your business.

Taking my passion and turning it into my work has been a thrilling transformation. I encourage anyone with a passion to give it a try. I'd like to restate the quote I started my article with...

Heart and soul are the wings of a business.
When you get it right, your business will soar.

Barbara Yager, the Happiness at Work Expert, builds company cultures filled with happy, engaged employees. Her passion is helping companies to zero in on their brand, culture, customers and employees with a heart-centered focus.

Barbara is a passionate and engaging business expert who specializes in building profitable organizational cultures. She puts her 22 plus years of business expertise to work finding the right solutions for her clients. Barbara believes that when a business has a clear picture of its Standards, Values and Attitudes, it will be very successful. Customers are drawn to businesses with heart. When you have plenty of happy customers, you will always have a robust bottom line.

Barbara offers free 30-minute consultations to prospective clients seeking a better way to do business. Contact her today for more information. Find out what adding a little heart and soul to your business can do. Visit Barbara's websites www.criglobalcaps.com or www.FindHappinessAtWork.com

Your customers will thank you!

"Purposeful action is what transforms people, communities and the world."
~ Norm Hull

Event Organizers Can Change the World, One "Hello" at a Time

Norm Hull

Purposeful action is what transforms people, communities and the world.

"You had me at Hello."

Imagine if the line Renee' Zellwegers's character had said to Tom Cruise in the movie Jerry McGuire was, "You lost me at Hello." How would the tone of that scene have played to the audience? The happy ending that everyone was hoping for would not have taken place. We would have left the movie theater frustrated, disappointed and thinking twice about ever going to see another romantic comedy. We knew they had a connection and it was summed up with her proclamation.

In my 35 years of speaking and presenting before audiences I have witnessed many colleagues, event organizers, lose their audience from crucial "touchpoint" moments that take place before the program ever begins. My clients, who have hired me to facilitate their events, have often expressed their appreciation when I use my tools and processes to increase the engagement, learning and retention among participants.

I work with clients who engage me at the beginning of their event planning; not at the execution stage. Being part of the process in the beginning provides the opportunity for me to utilize my years of experience and prevent common mistakes.

There are 3 reasons why you hire an event facilitator; to change a behavior, to create a feeling or to impart knowledge. I use my expertise to address each of the areas when it meets the needs of my clients. There are 3 common mistakes event organizers make which lead to poor evaluations, low participation and a reluctance to return. Allow me to offer some strategies to avoid those mistakes.

Strategy #1

Take the opportunity to create the ideal tone of the event.

Before the first presenter takes the stage, create a supportive environment for participants.

Are your participants sitting in their seats waiting for the "Welcome", that sounds like everyone else's beginning? "We are so glad you made it, we are going to have fun, learn a lot and now let's get started. First let me give you some housekeeping...blah, blah, blah. Now here is the introduction of our speaker....blah, blah."

Are they feeling like they are going to get anything different with this type of tone setting?

My clients recognize the value of having me as their event facilitator because they want to create an experience for the audience that entices, energizes, challenges and inspires them to learn and want to attend your next event.

One of the secrets to event success is keeping this thought in your head when planning, "How do we create an agenda with the components attendees love and provide value that makes our returning to our event next year, a 'no-brainer' choice? Your audience will gravitate to your future events if you have created an inclusive environment, meaningful activities and an agenda that enlightens as well as entertains."

Part of my expertise, as the event facilitator is addressing the thoughts going through the minds of participants.

How you answer the following questions can increase the value of your event to the participant:

- Are you going to have me meet others who are in the audience so I can create a connection that will get me someone to eat with at lunch since I know no one?

- Are you going to put me in group so I have an accountability partner who will make sure I am pro-active when seeking the information I need?

- Are you going to give me an opportunity to share my "Why" I am attending and what I need to take away from this event to validate attending again?

These are important questions your participants need to know the answers to when they arrive for your event.

When working with event organizers it is part of the critical conversations I have as we map out the audience experience.

Putting as much effort into the "first session" for the audience is where the "lost me at hello" mindset can be avoided. This session creates a warm, comfortable audience mindset before your speaker takes the stage.

Two action steps to include in every event you plan:

1. Leave room on the name badge for two bits of information besides the name: Space for "this is what I really do well in my business" and "this is where I need some additional support and why I am here."

2. Have them fill in the space so each time they meet someone, they can share their areas of strength and where they may offer their assistance. As the facilitator, I use this tool as a conversation starter before we begin the program.

Go to www.NormHull.com/SOS to download a sample of the name tag I use.

How many times have you attended the networking or social hour at an event and walked away feeling like there was more "connecting among the pre-existing cliques" or the people were not very social at all? There will always be introverts as well as extroverts in the room. Plan accordingly and don't leave it up to your participants to fend for themselves. The extroverts will be fine but most introverts will leave early or go do something else that's easier. This is another reason you need a facilitator to take the lead and have your people make the most of the gathering.

Imagine the increased value of attending your event when your participants easily share their expertise, build new relationships and have a great time engaging with peers. Changing the structure of these "standard/ staple components" provides great dividends before your speaker ever even takes the stage.

Every organizer wants participants to return to their next conference, right? Make sure you "have them at Hello." Seize the opportunity to create a welcoming environment so they will keep coming back.

You've found the best presenter and the location is great, so let's put some icing on the proverbial cake by creating a great tone for your audience.

Strategy #2

Create a structure where your audience takes responsibility for their own success.

Have you ever left an event or workshop feeling like you wasted your time and money because your expectations were not met?

Have your participants ever felt that way after leaving an event you organized?

Did the evaluations disappoint after you poured all your energy and soul into creating a great experience for your clients?

Wouldn't it be great if you could attend any event and know you would leave with what you wanted when you registered, GUARANTEED?

Here's my secret to making sure my audience members get what they need. I get them thinking about their intentions and what they need to take away from any session to make it worth their investment of time and money.

When I am facilitating, I have them write it down. They each share with a partner and I ask a few audience members to share with the large group. WHY? Because it now positions me to boomerang the responsibility on them and charge them with taking the proactive steps to have their intentions fulfilled.

"I am attending the 'We Can Make a Difference Conference' to find three inclusive activities to solve my companies multi-generational challenges which impact our bottom line. My intention is to leave with 5 options, a result of committing to meet making new connections."

This sounds better than "I was disappointed in the speaker, session or workshop. I didn't get what I hoped for."

They now have the mindset to seek out the answer or solution themselves. They have to put forth effort by talking to others in attendance, asking questions of presenters instead of hoping it gets covered.

Imagine 200 people at your event, each one with their own personal expectation. Is it realistic to have a presenter provide what they are all expecting?

An effective event facilitator keeps their audience accountable for their own self direction which makes for better participants and happier event organizers.

Go to http://www.normhull.com/selfsuccess where you can download my "Intention form" that I use with my audiences. I created the form in triplicate so the originator and their accountability partner each have a copy. The third copy is posted in the meeting room. When the intention has been fulfilled the originator pulls the copy down from the wall.

The benefit of this third, visible copy is it showcases fulfillment and action taken by participants. Posting of the form allows you, the event organizer, to be aware of what people are seeking.

This process takes place before the first speaker ever takes the stage creating the mindset for participants to take charge of their experience and seek out what they need. Activity is always better than passivity.

Strategy #3

Include an Event Facilitator as part of your program.

When I am hired as an Event Facilitator it is a

strategic action taken by the event organizer to create the ideal tone, increase event success and enhance the participants' experience. Hiring the ill-suited type of professional for this role is a common and costly mistake event organizers sometimes make when they fail to appreciate or recognize the value this position adds to the event.

One of the many skills I've mastered over the years is turning any hiccup in a program into a meaningful experience. When you add a message, lesson or point to ponder to any disruption, it becomes a "bonus learning lesson" that is positioned to support your overall focus.

I had a client who mistakenly announced the incorrect results of the election for the highest office of their association. Twenty minutes later she discovered her mistake and asked if I could help rectify the situation. Of course I told her I could and proceeded to preface the coming announcement with the appropriate learning experience that protected the dignity of all the parties involved. Was it easy? Nope, but because I was the facilitator, it was not about the client's mistake it was about the process and doing what was correct. Imagine an emcee hired for entertainment being asked to solve this crisis. Seasoned event planners recognize expert event facilitators are more than "crowd movers" and "announcers of housekeeping details." They hire us because we are their stealth asset, capable of filling the unexpected session opening, engaging the audience and solving unintended challenges that require more than playing a song loudly.

Consider this common example which takes place at many events.

The emcee, hired solely for entertainment purposes may start a general session off with loud "dance music" to "energize the audience."

Now before you get riled up, I like dancing and have been known to get down with my bad self. Dancing can be an energy elevator, time filler or a transitional tool. In most instances is it used to "artificially" raise the energy level of an audience. The music ends and a few minutes later the energy level returns to where it was originally.

The downside is... it is not usual for an audience to get frustrated when an emcee uses this energy raising resource, over and over and over. It seems to be the only tool they have so they overuse it, which reduces its effectiveness and builds resentment towards the emcee.

As an experienced event facilitator I use music and other energy raising tools sparingly and strategically. Any event facilitator worth their salt will incorporate any activity they ask the audience to participate in as part of the comprehensive event plan.

Action without meaning or purpose is usually

perceived as nothing more than filling time. You change your community, association or company when everyone understands the purpose and meaning behind every action. Purposeful action is what has always changed the world.

Audience management is part of the skills I have honed as an event facilitator.

You will recognize when you work with me, my underlying "WHY" for everything I do, suggest and include is so you will "Have them at Hello" and your event is successful.

My expert wisdom in creating great learning environments and personal experiences for any audience is why I am hired.

Hello, my name is Norm Hull and I turn their "goodbye" into "when is your next event?"

Norm Hull, CSP, is passionately committed to guiding leadership luminaries, entrepreneurs and coaches to success with their live events and client gatherings. Norm is the principal of Norm Hull & Associates, a personal development consulting company focusing primarily on teaching event organizers the Secret Sauce of Audience Mastery and Event Conversion Formula for transformative changes.

An acclaimed speaker, author and leadership expert, Norm has educated, entertained and inspired over 3,000,000 audience members with his programs. A snapshot of clients: PepsiCo, Jostens, YUM, Taco Bell, Pizza Hut, World Travel Inc, Disney, Universal Studios, Department of Defense, Ncredible Inc. and a long list of Educational Institutions and Associations.

Norm's greatest joy is being Grandpapa of two awesome grandchildren and the subject of many stories told by his friends and family. In his spare time Norm enjoys being part of the SYTA All Star Band, caretaker to his father and the ignored owner of a hybrid wolf. Connect with him at <u>NormHull.com</u>

*A true mentor believes in you before you
believe in yourself.*
~ Noah St. John

The Science and Soul of Words

Tanya Villar

There is science in your words and soul in your tone!

Before your eyes open, the alarm clock is nudging you to wake up... a mili-moment passes and "boom" there it is... the initial feeling of your day.... "is it Monday, oh yeah, its Monday... ugh.. I hate Monday." "I wish it was Friday.... Get your butt up... God I hope there's coffee...."

That initial feeling.... that E-motion.... the very first one of your day sets the tone for the hours that follow. Isn't it interesting that if the alarm goes off at 3 am, so that you can catch your plane to an exotic island for vacation; your initial feeling of your day and the dialog that follows would be quite different?

Have you ever wanted to have the power to FEEL amazing each moment and FEEL that amazingness of who you are every day? The secret is in listening with intent to what you are saying to yourself and understanding the Science and Soul of your words.

Our words are the logical beginning point to re-programming our habitual negative self-talk. Establishing *Authentic Soul Speak* as the first voice we hear in the morning is a sign that we are living and experiencing a life rich with joy and fulfillment. *Our inner voices* can be best described by the illustration of the "good angel" on one shoulder and the "bad angel" on the other. Our *Authentic Soul Speak* is a voice beyond the dialog of "good" and "bad." As Rumi quotes, *"Beyond our ideas of right doing and wrong doing there is a field; I'll meet you there."* We really reside beyond the conflict of our minds.

Chris Young sings *"I hear voices all the time."* As his song *"Voices"* details; most of our internal voices are echoes of memories. Some of the voices are rehearsed conversations, some of them are soothing. For the most part when we seek peace, we are seeking our internal dialog to be still so that we can connect to the deeper meaning of our lives. We all feel that deep inside; we are amazing people with divine talents connected to our purpose. Remember the last time you held a new born baby, that feeling of awe and "speechlessness," the feeling of pure love and potential? Then, the conversation of our inner world shows up as ".... Ugh, it's Monday... ugh... I hate Mondays; I wish it was Friday... Get your butt up... God, I hope there's coffee..."

This stimulus response/automatic internal dialog used to greet me each morning. Today I am free from feeling trapped by this type of dialog and I teach others how to find their way to their own *Authentic Soul Speak* and the field of oneness. A wealthy life of bliss and freedom can be yours sooner rather than later. If you are ready to take that journey, be prepared to adopt some new habits for the next 40 consecutive days.

Forty days is KEY! The newest research in brain science has shown that this is the length of time it takes for new neuropathways to develop. Permanent change is the result of developing a new perception about your life. During this time, you will LISTEN to the "words" and "E-motions" of your inner dialog. You listen with the intention of seeing, feeling and embracing who you really are…. You are Divine!

Over the next 40 days, expect to increase your awareness of two main components; your exact words AND your primary E-motions. Your exact words will show you what you are focusing on, and more importantly your E-motions show you what you are "expecting" to occur.

Again, establishing a "Divine E-motional Perception" of yourself and your life is the doorway to a Quantum Shift.

The victory of every well-loved fairy tale and spiritual story is when the hero or heroine faces and defeats the "Demon" guarding their riches and true love. The secret to their success stems from their ability to connect to their TRUE NATURE. From their authentic self, the Hero/Heroine is capable of amazing, bold actions that lead to Money and Life Freedom.

Throughout our life stories, we have imagined a myriad of "Monsters" and our E-Motions feed them keeping them strong and alive. To illustrate this point I love the story of how lions hunt. Lions divide themselves into two groups; the young lions with sharp teeth and the old toothless lions. After they choose their hunting grounds, the groups separate. The young lions hide at one end of the hunting grounds and the old lions sit at the other end. When they are all in position, the old toothless lions begin to ROAR! The frightened animals run away from the ROAR right into the sharp teeth of the young hungry lions. The moral of this story is RUN TOWARD THE ROAR, IT HAS NO TEETH.

Lack of faith in yourself and being stuck *wanting* to REALLY create the life of your dreams is the result of running from uncomfortable E-motions. In doing so, the pain is multiplied and fear based actions and decisions take over. Rather, we are meant to be led by the peace, wisdom and wealth of our SOUL. If at this time in your life you have exhausted attempts to create the life of your dreams, more than likely it is because you are spending time, energy and money running *away* from your ROAR.

Emotions commonly associated with money and wealth creation are stress, worry and hoping to get lucky. These E-motions are also coupled with guilt and shame because you "should" know better or you "should" have more money, more happiness or be debt free by NOW! Emotions drive your thoughts each morning when you awake. The thoughts that follow drive your decisions and your actions throughout your day. Simply stated your Emotions are ENERGY in MOTION. E-Motions are the fuel of every action we create, therefore Mastery of your E-motions is key to ENJOYING your life. Once you have practiced feeling and loving each and every E-motion, then you are FREE to fuel your life with the E-motions you choose.

There is no greater agony than bearing an untold story inside of you. ~ Maya Angelou

Here is the process for releasing those untold stories:

To begin, choose a specific journal for your 40 days. I always write my intention for my 40 days within the front cover. I love re-reading my journals, and each time I do, I am amazed how what I asked for has manifested. I have completed over forty 40 Day Money and Life Freedom Journeys since 2010!

During my first 40 day experience, I intended to meet my soul mate, I met him on day 23 of my 40 days. He is now my amazing husband.

My second 40 days, I intended to be a New York Times best-selling author, on day 24 I received a call to teach Money and Life Freedom to the "Passion Test" team! With that team, I am well on my way to creating a best seller. After experiencing the most amazing, predictable results, I teamed up with Jane Cabrera and Beth Lefevre to share this process worldwide. Your journal will also serve as a valuable record keeping system for your progress.

Over the next 40 Days you will establish "intentional loving actions" towards yourself through doing the following daily practices.

1. Authentic Journaling is Free Flow writing – All is Divine.

2. Run toward your Roar - Free Flow Emotions.

3. Discernment – Are you Running Away? Moving Toward?

4. Begin each day and end each night Speaking Sweet Words to yourself.

1. Authentic Journaling

Journaling is a body mind exercise that helps to access the subconscious mind. It also allows you to look at your thoughts objectively and detach from them.

Each day, I prefer morning, however I have discovered that the discipline of *when* I journal is not as important as the discipline of journaling daily.

Create at least 15 minutes of time for yourself to do a "brain, emotional release" onto paper. Write at the speed of your authentic feelings at the moment you are writing. This practice strengthens your ability to express authentically in the now. It also increases your awareness of the E-motions you are utilizing to move within your day.

After you have written all you FEEL compelled to write, close your eyes, and take a few deep breaths.

Next step is to re-read what you wrote and notice any words and or phrases that you used repeatedly. Attending to your exact words will assist you in re-focusing your perception on what is true and divine instead of what is a "memory."

Specifically re-read your entry and extract the following:
- Repetitive words and/or short phrases
- Any I AM statements

- List the main emotions felt

Doing this daily over a period of time will reveal a pattern of thoughts and feelings that lead to the creation of *emotional expectation of a specific outcome.* Simply stated, you will see clearly the Emotions and outcome you are running away from.

2. Running Toward the Roar Practice

Now it is time to allow your E-motions to be felt and honored.

It's time to ramp up the E-motions giving yourself permission to have and feel them.

Validate your feelings by saying things such as: *I feel as if I am a failure.*

Then follow it up with the truth: *and I am Magnificent.*

The purpose is to come to a place of peace that will come within the first 3 days after doing this exercise. You will feel peace.

Adding the "I am Magnificent," opens a neuro processor in your brain allowing you to feel both Emotions at the same time. 'I am' statements have more power than 'I feel' statements and will override them over time.

Over 40 days, this practice with prove to create a marked improvement and increase of feeling supported, peace, harmony and connectedness which is also known as 'being in the flow.' The feeling of peace will encourage you to continue this practice.

Right around day 20 will come the "pivotal day" where you may feel yourself wanting to quit. When in actuality, your breakthrough is right around the corner. I suggest you take a nap. Sleep is essential for releasing old connections and mapping a pathway to your money and life freedom.

Important note: during this phase, do NOT make any major life decisions. Do not sign any legal documents or agreements. Hold on for step 3 of the process.

3. Strengthen your Discernment

When faced with a decision during your 40 days, ask yourself this master discernment question, "Is this moving me toward my intention or is it moving me away?" Ponder this.

Then ask;

- If I take this action will I be moving toward my intention or will I be running away from something?

For example:

My intention:

- Multiply my Health and Vitality.

My moment of discernment:
- A bowl of M&Ms.

My internal dialog after realizing I have already eaten a handful of said M&Ms:
- "Tanya, what are you doing?"

My E-motion(s):
- Guilt
- Shame
- Oh no, big mistake.

My Discernment Practice:
- Slow down – 3 deep breaths.
- Allow the feelings of guilt, shame to flow.
- Journal freely.
- Re-read my words from an emotional feeling of peace.
- Lovingly ask myself: "What E-motion am I running away from?"

My Discovery:
- The moment I was overeating candy I was writing this chapter.
- At the moment I reached for the second handful of M&Ms, I realized I was masking the feeling of uncertainty.

My Freedom:
- Relaxing into the E-motions of uncertainty.
- I am feeling uncertain AND I am magnificent.
- Now I am free to choose what I eat, when I eat, instead of being compelled to cover up an E-motion.

4. Speak lovingly to yourself

Sweet words and tones spoken to yourself is an easy transformative daily practice.

Each morning as you awake and each night as you lay your head on your pillow speak loving, encouraging words to yourself. Remember the awe you felt the last time you held and spoke to a newborn baby.

Now realize this: You are a newborn with years of experience. How precious and amazing and awe inspiring you have become!

I have created a 40 day journal outline for you to use. Simply go to http://thesouthernmuse.com to download your copy. It is designed with soul provoking guidance, inspirational quotes and as always, is filled with much love and honor for you on your journey!

67

Tanya Villar, the Southern Muse, believes that the art of authentic living is the highest reflection of self-love. Her passion for education and embracing individuality in the beauty of oneness has taken her on her own soul's journey. During the last 30 years, Tanya has passionately studied the quantum physics of change, ancient spiritual texts and the leading edge science of neuroplasticity.

Tanya's passion for transformation has brought her to guiding men and women to reclaim themselves through self-love while bringing beauty and freedom into authentic living. Her transformational programs use the science and soul of words and compassionate communication to support them through the process of unblocking key areas of life. Through the integration of this learning, practical results are measurable and fun. Life is meant to be lived spontaneously and joyfully.

For more information on how you can master the art of authentic living, go to www.thesouthernmuse.com or contact Tanya at Tanya@thesouthernmuse.com.

"Success is in the moment, make every moment count."
~ Omar Periu

Rules of Engagement: The Top Ten Unwritten Skills of Success

Judy Ann Michael, MBA

Your success is my passion.

Throughout my 30-year career, both as an entrepreneur and in corporate America, I've been fortunate to have mentors who shared success skills that weren't taught in business school, but have been vital to my career. Since we often learn best through examples, I'll describe these rules in a short story that's fictional, yet all too true.

Rules of Engagement

Jean Frazier, Marketing Vice President, slumped into her office chair after another brutal meeting. Her employer, CanineMedica, had just laid off 25% of their employees, including her entire marketing staff. Despite the loss of her team, the CEO still expected Jean to launch the company's most innovative product, Zeela, a super-premium dog food for senior dogs, in the next 90 days. Jean firmly believed in the product, and used the first samples on her own geriatric dog, Joshua, watching him come to life with the healthy doses of nutrients and natural anti-inflammatory ingredients for his arthritic hips. Jean felt strongly that Zeela could support the growing niche market of senior dogs, and her CEO expected a highly successful product launch of Zeela to save CanineMedica's bottom line.

Jean received approval to spend $20,000 on contractors over the next 90 days, and she'd spend every penny of it on creative marketing expertise. Her CEO also threw in an $18,000 bonus if sales of Zeela reached the national audience their analysis told them was out there. Jean had a soft spot in her heart for dogs, but was a Tiger Lady when it came to reaching her sales goals.

Jean scoured her LinkedIn contacts, searching for a trusted contact who'd have a marketing wiz referral. She stumbled upon Liz Hightower, the Chief Marketing Officer at the local electric utility company. Liz's company received an award for their innovative web campaign targeted at saving energy, so Jean decided to give Liz a call.

"Mandy Wallen, my former senior creative designer, left last year to start her own business, Assensia Marketing. She could help you," offered Liz.

"Liz, will I be able to count on her?" asked Jean. "After 30 years in this business, we've seen a lot of people come and go. I need someone I can trust."

"She'll definitely need coaching, Jean, but her content is awesome. She's the reason why we won the Excellence in Marketing award," said Liz.

Assensia Marketing's website had some of the most compelling visuals Jean had ever seen. The images showed emotionally gripping content yet had a flair for customer engagement and product promotion. Jean hoped she could leverage Assensia's creativity for Zeela's target audience of Baby Boomers, a geriatric dog-loving population who had the disposable income to pay $65.00 for a bag of dog food.

Jean dialed the number listed on the website, and the call went direct to voicemail. She heard, "It's me. Leave a message." Jean was unsure by the generic greeting if she'd reached Assensia, but left a quick message with her project needs and contact information and requested an urgent callback.

It was nearly midnight when Jean crawled into bed. Hoping for sleep after a grueling day, she heard her cell phone buzzing unexpectedly. Assuming an emergency, she answered.

"This is Mandy. You called?"

Jean was shocked at the late night phone call, and unsure of Mandy's definition of ASAP. "Are you Mandy from Assensia Marketing?" Jean asked.

"Yeah."

Jean was taken aback by Mandy's glib answer, but continued. "Liz Hightower recommended you. I work for CanineMedica and I'm looking for a marketing contractor. She spoke highly of your award-winning creativity."

"I liked Liz," responded Mandy. "Had to leave that place though. What a grind."

Jean's gut was telling her to hang up, but she continued. "I understand you offer creative marketing services?"

"Yep. That's me."

"Mandy, were you able to look at CanineMedica's website?" Jean asked. "Do you know who we are?"

"Haven't had the time to look."

Jean decided to take control of the conversation lest it continue its aimless course. "Mandy, I hear great things about your work. Do you have the capacity to take on a large project?"

"Maybe. I could use the money," said Mandy.

Jean agreed with Liz's recommendation about coaching. Mandy might know marketing, but didn't know business, and definitely knew nothing about serving customers.

Jean asked, "Mandy, can you meet me at my office tomorrow at 2 p.m.?"

"I guess so," said Mandy flatly.

"Thanks," said Jean. "See you at 2 p.m."

Jean put down her phone and sat down next to

her sleepy pooch. "You know, Joshua, Mandy hasn't learned the Rules of Engagement yet," Jean said as she nuzzled Joshua's warm head. *"**Rule #1 is to be Professional**. I hope she can be more courteous in person than she was on the phone!"*

Jean dreaded going into the office after yesterday's traumatic news. After three meetings, four tearful conversations and six urgent phone calls, she realized that it was 2:15 p.m. and Mandy was a no-show. By 2:30, Jean had given up, and started outlining Plan B to find a marketing contractor.

At 2:45, the receptionist announced Mandy's arrival. Jean entered the lobby, and eyed a young woman who conveyed a look of shaky confidence. "I'm Mandy. From Assensia?"

Jean eyed the 20-something woman, was impressed by her professional dress and handshake, but not happy about her late arrival. "Maybe she's just a diamond in the rough," Jean pondered.

"I'm Jean. Glad to meet you," Jean said. She led Mandy down the hallway to her office and offered Mandy a seat.

Jean wondered why there was no apology for Mandy's tardiness. ***Rule #2: Be on time*** came to mind. Jean remembered being yelled at by a high-profile client early in her career for being five minutes late to a meeting. She was never late again.

"So tell me what you know about CanineMedica," Jean said.

"It looks like you sell dog food," Mandy said as she shifted in her chair. "I didn't really have time to look."

Jean remembered being a newbie at a consulting firm. Her first manager taught her ***Rule #3: Know the Customer.*** "You can't help them until you know them," her Manager drilled into her. Jean took great pains to research her clients so she could ask questions, listen, learn, and solve problems.

Jean asked, "Tell me, Mandy, why did you start your own business?"

Mandy shifted in her chair. "I don't really like having a boss, so I decided to work for myself."

Jean stifled her desire to laugh out loud. Working for yourself just means you answer to your customer, not a superior with a title. Jean had discovered that in the nine years of owning her own consulting business. ***Rule #4: Whoever writes the checks IS the boss.***

Mandy felt she was more of a night person and didn't like the rigidity of working 8 to 5. She wanted to work whenever she wanted so her creative juices could easily flow.

"She must've been feeling creative at midnight last night so she called me," Jean thought. ***Rule***

#5: *Do what it takes to get the job done*. Jean remembered complaining to a manager long ago about the 70-hour work weeks they endured for urgent consulting client projects. "There are no regular business hours, Jean, just the hours it takes to deliver a great product," he told her. Jean found his advice applied to her entrepreneurial business and as the leader of a corporate marketing department.

"Mandy, did you bring any work samples?" Jean asked. She doubted Mandy's work ethic, but wanted a closer look at her marketing portfolio.

"I can invite you to my Facebook page," Mandy responded.

Jean's heart sank. This could have been a slam-dunk agreement. Show me your work, read our website, and sign a contract for $20,000. But Mandy's lack of preparation made it difficult for Jean to clearly see if Mandy could truly solve the marketing challenge that lay in front of her. ***Rule #6: Be prepared and make it easy for the client to say yes.***

"Mandy, how much do you usually charge for your services?" Jean asked.

Mandy took a moment to think about it. "I guess it depends on the project. I think $1,500 would work for this project."

Jean quickly did the math in her head and realized that Mandy had agreed to earn roughly

$3.00 an hour. Jean knew that if you don't know the scope of what you need to do, and what you'll put into it, you'll end up hating every minute of it. ***Rule #7: Know your numbers,*** or you'll regret it.

Jean got up from her chair and gazed out the window. It would take time to mentor this young artistic genius with no business skills into a successful young entrepreneur. Alternatively, Jean could waste time searching for another resource who may not have the time or talent she needed, and blow her $20,000 budget.

A framed picture of Joshua, her aging pooch with bad hips, caught her eye. Jean thought of the thousands of other dogs who could benefit from Zeela. She gently grasped the picture and handed it to Mandy.

"Mandy, do you like dogs?" Jean asked. "This is my Joshua. He's a 12-year-old rescue dog with arthritis. And Zeela helps him get through the day with less pain."

Mandy put her hand across her heart. "Last month I lost my Black Lab, Sam, to hip dysplasia. He was 9 years old. It was horrible." A tear came to her eye. "I never want to go through that again."

Rule 8: All great teams have a common vision of success. Jean had worked with geniuses, misfits, nobodies, and experts. As long as they all believed in what they were doing, magic could, and did, happen.

Jean weighed the odds, and decided to bet on Mandy and her ability to learn the Rules of Engagement and become an expert in her field. "Mandy, I want you to come back tomorrow at 8 a.m. You're going to be on time, and bring samples of five client projects. You're going to read every last page of our website, along with detailed material I'll give you on our new product. You're going to have to work all night to get ready, but if you're prepared, I think we can come to a mutually agreeable contract. Are you up for it?"

Mandy straightened up in her chair, and her shaky self-confidence was gone. "This is so cool! I can already see using Joshua as part of the campaign! Can I borrow your picture for a test ad?"

Jean could tell Mandy believed in the project and could immediately make a contribution. There might be hope after all.

Jean cringed, thinking of the time in her mid-30s when she'd royally screwed up a project from good intentions and lack of experience. Luckily, she'd had a great mentor who taught her **Rule #9: *If you believe in someone, give her a second chance.***

Jean silently thanked the mentors who'd challenged her to learn and practice the Rules of Engagement. They'd corrected her mistakes and taught her to do better and hone her expertise.

As Mandy excitedly reached to shake her hand, Jean remembered ***Rule 10: Teach what you know and help others be successful.*** She hoped Mandy would learn these rules. They'd be a great complement to her creative skills and would help her realize her potential. And someday, Mandy might pass along the Rules of Engagement to the next naïve genius who called at midnight and contribute to the next generation of successful business experts.

Conclusion

You may wonder if these Rules are effective, so I challenge you to answer this question. For those experts you know who have a track record of long-term success, how many of them are late, rude, clueless about their customers, financially unaware, unfocused and self-centered? Probably none. True, lasting success comes from focusing your talents, growing your business, partnering with your customers, working towards a vision, and contributing to the achievement of others. Practicing these Rules establishes integrity and trust. Living these Rules builds expertise and wisdom to be shared with others.

Judy Ann Michael specializes in using proven, simplified strategies to develop collaborative solutions for business success. For over 25 years, Judy has worked closely with the nation's largest firms to enhance profits, and now brings that experience to help small and medium size businesses thrive in today's ever changing and competitive business world. She's helped develop profitable solutions for UPS, Cedars Sinai Medical Center, T-Mobile, and developed business strategies to drive growth in multiple industries.

Judy assists firms in crafting specific, strategic

action plans that put them on the road to realizing their short and long term goals. She brings her wealth of consulting expertise to support small and medium size business owners compete in an ever growing and complex market, using simple tools and great advice to ensure success.

Strategicactionsolutions.com

The Pathway to Productive Change

Michael Jenkins

Focus first and results follow.

How can you make change happen when there so many distractions all around you? Distractions compete for your time, your money and your very soul. We all have them and sometimes we welcome them. But the question is do we invite them consciously or do we permit distraction to range freely? The sad truth is that many times we are not aware that we are allowing distraction freedom.

I grew up in South Central Los Angeles in the late sixties, and I graduated from high school in the early seventies. My family could not afford to send me to college. Beyond that, I am not even sure I could qualify to attend college academically.

After I graduated, I spent a year wandering aimlessly and finding work at fast food restaurants, like McDonald's and Jack-in-the-Box. In a short time, something inside me was begging for a change. I thought a change of environment, for sure, would help. I certainly wanted no part of being in gangs.

Gangs were a part of living and growing up for young black males in South Central Los Angeles. The attraction was as much about a feeling of belonging as it was the need to feel protected. Gang life also included the presence of drugs and violence. Fortunately for me, I knew gang life was not an option for me. I also knew that, if didn't make the right moves, life would still be tough.

My oldest brother had escaped the gang life. He enlisted in the United States Air Force. That was huge and I knew I would miss him. He had always encouraged me to follow him and to do many of the things he enjoyed doing. But for some reason military enlistment was not one of the things he encouraged me to do. Perhaps he wanted to keep me far away from any of the conflict in Vietnam.

Nevertheless, his decision inspired me. His enlistment took him far away from South Central and gave him new opportunities. It was a smart move. So, when I was old enough, I decided to enlist, like my brother. I made the decision to enlist in the United States Navy. It was the first time I had decided to go my own way.

The Navy was my ticket to the change I was seeking. I thought it would be like the saying, "Join the Navy, and see the world." This idea of traveling to new places really excited me. I could leave

South Central Los Angeles and travel around the world. What made it more exciting was that I would receive education and training to work in the medical field as a hospital corpsman. And I would qualify for the G.I. Bill to pay for college after discharge from the service. My future looked very promising.

Everything seemed to be going my way. After attending boot camp at the Naval Training Center, San Diego, my first duty station was the Navy Hospital Corpsman School – San Diego. I was to attend the school's 14 week program, then graduate as an esteemed Hospital Corpsman. The program was comprehensive, covering topics such as anatomy and physiology, first aid, trauma wound care, and more.

Corpsmen are specially trained for the critical job of caring for wounded or sick sailors and Marines. Needless to say, it is important to pay attention in the classroom and to exercise good study habits. The goal, of course, is to become knowledgeable and well prepared to address all medical situations and emergencies.

Yes, the goal was clear, but I was very distracted. As happy as I was to enlist in the Navy, I was now happy to feel the freedom that came after 8 weeks of restriction in boot camp. I was 18 and thought it was time I started enjoying my new life. I was on my own, in a new city, new people, new everything.

I let my new freedom be the cause for me to lose focus in my training. My grades slipped dramatically and I faced being dropped from the program. Initially, I did not take this to be a serious possibility. It wasn't until I was called in to meet with a school administrator that I paid attention. The message I received was delivered with great clarity. I would be dropped from the program and forced to take a job I did not want. I would have no choice in the matter if I was dropped from the program.

Fortunately I was able to convince the administrator to give me another chance. I was scared. I did *not* want to leave the program. The threat was that I would be assigned to a ship to work as a Boatswain's Mate. That was not what I wanted to do. That said, I need to be clear that every job in the Navy is essential to the defense of our country. But the job I signed up for was Hospital Corpsman, nothing else.

So, I knew I had to get more focused. I would have to eliminate the distractions. And, there were many of them. As I began to really think about why I was so distracted, I learned the main reason for the distractions was all in my head. I really didn't believe in myself and was convinced that I could not have the life I imagined. My eyes were now wide open. It was important that I learn to believe in my best self; to turn things around and continue my Hospital Corpsman training this was necessary for me.

"There are two major pains in life. One is the pain of discipline; the other is the pain of regret. Discipline weighs ounces, but regret weighs tons when you allow your life to drift along unfulfilled."
~ Jim Rohn

I'll share more about my journey a little later. Today, I believe that believing in our best selves is a struggle for many people. It is a reason that we seem to take one step forward and three steps back. We sabotage our own progress. It happens all the time when we try new ways of doing things. We may give up too early and allow negative self-talk to run amok.

Sometimes we must make sacrifices, or what I call **productive changes**. These are changes that require focused action or activity. I had to learn what to concentrate on what to let go of. It was as necessary for me as it will be for you to focus on the mission-critical activities.

What are mission-critical activities? They are activities that are defined and specific. Performing these types of activities will lead you to the desired outcome or result.

An example would be the mission-critical

activities necessary to achieve the desired result of losing weight. Some of the activities might include drinking eight glasses of water a day, exercising one hour a day, eating six small meals a day, and sleeping a minimum of seven hours a night. They are considered mission-critical because, if they are not done as prescribed, the results may be delayed or never realized.

Let's look at another example that has a business perspective. The one that comes to mind is the general idea of selling more to increase your income. The over-reaching activity is selling. But let's take it a few steps further and get more specific. What are the mission-critical activities involved in making sales?

Here is a list of the commonly accepted activities involved in sales work:

- Prospecting or targeting the right client group or demographic.
- Qualifying prospects to learn if your product or service will have value to them.
- Presenting the features and benefits of your product offering.
- Following up to build relationships and move the sales process forward.
- Responding to prospect concerns or objections, and closing or finalizing the order.

Do you think that if a person focuses on doing these activities and doesn't give in to distraction they will see the results they want? Yes, the odds are more in favor of their achieving the desired outcome. It does not matter who you are or where you come from. When you get focused, the right doors open up. It makes no difference whether the change you want to make is personal or business related.

Here's the message: what we focus on expands. It has also been said that our energy flows where our attention goes. Both ideas explain why focus is the pathway to productive change. If we focus on distractions or give our energy to activities that do not support changes we want to make, we are doomed. But when we focus on the mission-critical activities required to make productive change, we can prepare to celebrate our wins.

Try it for yourself. Decide what you want, where you want to go or what you want to do. I am sure you know it helps to be specific. This gives you the framework you need to select or identify your mission-critical activities.

The final step is to do the work. Let me illustrate what I mean with a quick story of the Three Frogs. There are three frogs in a pond and each frog is sitting on a lily pad. One of the frogs decides to jump. How many frogs are left sitting on a lily pad? Logically, we all know that if one of the frogs decided to jump off its lily pad, two remain on a lily pad. People are usually surprised, and perhaps you are as well when you hear that all three frogs are left sitting on top of lily pads. The story says that one frog *decided* to jump. It didn't say that it actually jumped.

The point of the story is that decisions we make are not always followed by action. You must act on your decision and do the work.

Now, to finish my story . . .

I hunkered down and got busy doing what I needed to do to finish my training. It was hard but worth it. My greatest work was to change what was happening between my ears. I had to learn to believe that it was possible for me to do something I didn't truly believe was possible. I decided I wanted to succeed and become a Navy Corpsman. I also realized the opportunity for me was now. It was amazing. No longer were the distractions winning. Yes, I was required to follow orders as a member of the U.S. Military. But, I was given the chance to have a say in my future and it was important that I not give it away.

I got focused. I determined what my mission-critical activities were. They included prioritizing time for study, meeting with classmates to discuss and review material and lessons, and paying real attention in class. It sounds simple, right? It was anything but simple. After all, the things I allowed to distract me before were still out there and calling for my attention.

What I later realized was that I learned to focus my energies towards the results I desired. This was indeed a positive and productive change for me. My decision was fueled with action, and I graduated from the program on time and never gave another thought to the idea of doing another job during my time in the Navy.

The lessons I learned helped me throughout my six-year Navy career. I became a unit leader and senior Corpsman. The experience has also served me well as civilian. I know with absolute certainty that focus can be your pathway for productive change.

Do it now.
What change do you want to make?
Be bold.

~~~~~~

A Letter of Appreciation from the Commanding Officer to Michael Jenkins

On the occasion of your release from active duty, I wish to express my sincere appreciation for your outstanding performance of duty.

You easily adapted and performed well in all your assignments. Your superb performance of duty is particularly noteworthy as you easily and expertly made the transition from a general duty corpsman to that of a skilled neuropsychiatric technician. You have been dedicated, consistent and highly motivated for further improvement for yourself and others. As senior corpsman on the closed psychiatric unit, you have been skillful in managing in an excellent leadership role.

It is with great pleasure that I extend my personal thanks and best wishes for happiness and continued success in your future endeavors.

D. Earl Brown, Jr.
Rear Admiral, Medical Corps
United States Navy

Michael Jenkins is president and founder of Intelligent Leader Solutions, LLC and creator of Productive Change Management – a program which helps leaders and organizations manage productive tension to increase overall productivity. Michael has over 30 years of experience working with individuals and organizations helping to execute new initiatives using productive change strategies. He is a certified mastermind executive coach, a board certified coach and a master practitioner of the ChangeWorks® System. A graduate of San Diego State University, he also attended the University of

Phoenix for a master's degree in Organizational Management. Michael is also a proud U.S. Navy veteran and was a trained specialist in "neuropsychiatric healthcare." He grew up in South Central Los Angeles, and now lives in beautiful San Diego, California with his girl, Sandy.

Website:
www.productivechangemanagement.com
Email:
michael@productivechangemanagement.com

Becoming Conscious in an Unconscious World

Dolores Fazzino

When you show up in your life, magic happens!

Imagine: You are at a point in your life where you have hit the wall. Your life, which had been working for you, suddenly is no longer fulfilling or exciting, but is rather boring and stagnant. It seems like your life is no longer working for you. It feels as if you are on a hamster wheel, going through the motions of your day, living your life on other people's terms, and not your own. And you ask yourself, "Is this all there is? Where are the passion, the joy, the fun and fulfillment that I so desire?"

Your relationships start falling apart, you are no longer feeling fulfilled with life in general. Your career or job has changed in some form. Either the company is changing to meet the demands of society or through their bottom line or pocketbook. Or maybe the company is becoming more regulated and oblivious to what is important for their workers. You are now expected to do things that may not be in integrity with your values and ideals. You may have been notified that your job no longer exists, or you have been let go or disposed of since you no longer "fit in" with the company's values and goals. Everything seems to be coming to a head as if a volcano is about to erupt.

It is celebration time! For every situation, no matter how big, bad or insurmountable it may seem, there is an opportunity for something even better to come forth, maybe something that you find fulfilling or are passionate about. Whatever the reason, I invite you to welcome and embrace the ever evolving concept of change. Change has been and will continue to be the constant. You have now awakened on some level of your beingness. This is where the magic happens, when you have woken up and become a conscious participant in your life. When you are creating from a conscious and awakened state of being, that is called showing up in your life. Synchronicity and opportunities start manifesting. It is as if your life is flowing effortlessly. This is not about constantly doing or pushing a boulder up a mountain. It is about being. Many of us have no clue on how we can actually just BE.

A space needed to be created to allow something else to enter. When we are unconscious to this, the universe provides us with the changes we need to redirect us on our path. This is where quantum physics comes in. Leaving a situation such as a job or relationship creates a void. The universe will fill up this void with something else. The key is to be awake or conscious as to what you would like to fill that empty space with. It may be a new career or a new relationship or anything else you would like to create for yourself. It may also be to just be with whatever has happened until the inspiration comes to move to what will be next.

Did you know that many people move through their lives as walking "zombies" just like the walking dead? No passion, stuck, acting and looking rather scary. This is what happens when we are not living our life on our terms, living our passion, or not being our true authentic self. We just exist, not thriving or barely surviving. We are born to LIVE in authenticity.

Sometimes we have given our power away to another person, authority, following money or to an external force, something that is outside of ourselves. Doing this was most likely an unconscious choice. The norm of society has been to look for your happiness on the outside of yourself. How is that working for you?

Let's go back a bit in recent history, around the time of the 2008 economic bust. It seems that life had been quite predictable prior to 2008; you could bet your paycheck that things were pretty constant and had been for a long time. This created the illusion of stability. Then suddenly things changed overnight. It was as if the proverbial rug got pulled out from the majority of people both domestically and internationally. Anything that had an inkling of being stable outside of us was no longer stable.

Since then, there has been more flux and change, very similar to putting a load of laundry in the washer, going through the spin cycle and something rather different has emerged from the washer. Ever since 2008, there really has been no external stability. I also believe that many people affected by this received a wake-up call that it was time to take their power back. Those who had been unconscious, are now conscious and awake, realizing what had been, was no longer going to work and there was a *need* to take back their power. Yet, they did not know what that was or what it looked like. Many started their journey of personal growth and exploration of discovering who they are, and realized that the only stability that can be created is the stability that we feel from within us. It cannot be found outside of us, that's the illusion. I believe that this was an important pivotal point in humanity's evolution.

So how does one create inner stability? There are many paths to manifest this for ourselves.

1). Most importantly, live a heart-centered life.

This is where you are being true to yourself, being authentic and genuine. It is focusing on and bringing our energy through your heart. When you are in your heart space, you are in present moment, you are in your physical body, and you are experiencing life through your feelings.

Interestingly, many of us do not experience or feel your emotions. We would rather avoid them at all costs. Many of us think we are experiencing emotions, but in reality we are intellectualizing them. We have shut down the feeling part of ourselves, our heart space. Our heart space becomes isolated, protected by a self-created fortress of walls that sometimes the light of day does not even shine through. We have shut down emotionally to survive. This is because we may have experienced the unpleasantness of some of these emotions at one time or another and would rather not "go there" again. This avoidance of "going there" creates more issues for ourselves than you can ever imagine. We expend more energy trying to control and avoid going there than we do by actually experiencing the emotions. It becomes exhausting. No wonder many of us are under stress, have created illnesses for ourselves and are not very happy. That is where our minds come in. We are remembering what this felt like in the past, were afraid of what we experienced, and will do anything to avoid this from happening again. We are coming from a fear-based reality.

To shift a fear-based reality is simple. Everything in life is based upon simple concepts. It is us humans who make things more complicated, in particular the ego. The ego thrives to survive at any cost. The ego will make up stories, which may not be true to sway you. We also know that whatever you continue to focus on, you will create for yourself. This is a known fact with quantum physics and the laws of manifestation. So a viscous cycle is created and constantly continues to spiral out of control due to the fact the fear-based reality is being focused on. So now it is time to flip the switch to something directly opposite of fear: LOVE.

One of the easiest ways to move out of fear is to focus on the word LOVE. All words have a vibrational energetic component to them. For example, fear is heavy and has a low vibration; whereas love, is lighter and has a higher frequency to it. When you focus on the word LOVE and repeat it as a mantra, your energy will automatically raise itself. As with quantum physics, like attracts like. As you are raising your energy and frequency by repeating LOVE, anything that is not the same energetic frequency will fall away and may possibly disappear completely.

It really is as simple as that. In invite you to experiment with this and experience it for yourself, it is truly magical!

2). Realize that change is the new constant or normal.

Embrace change; consider it a new adventure or new and exciting chapter in your life! We are fortunate to have witnessed many amazing changes, innovations and processes in a rather short period of time. Just look at what has transpired in the field of electronics and social media! And know that it will only be consistently faster as time marches on.

For those of us who like to control things, change throws us curve ball. Our ego wants to have things just right and perfect in a nice neat package or box. Then change happens, and the box gets damaged. We are trying to get the box back to being perfect so that everything will be the same, yet the box will never be the same. Change will happen no matter if we dig our heels in and refuse to move forward or if we relax into the change. You can either move with the flow or resist the current; the outcome will be the same.

Sometimes there are hidden jewels or clues in

what we write. Our conscious thoughts and beliefs may surface and may shed some light on things. If thinking about change gives you the hives, I invite you to make a list of what you do not like about change.

Remember we *always* have choices in our decisions. Yes, that is true! Everything that we experience in life is based on a choice that we have made. Some of these choices are unconscious choices, and some are very conscious choices. And with every choice, there are end results based on these choices.

And lastly, remember that your attitude will create your reality.

3). Attitude is everything, and creates your reality.

Whatever you focus your attention on, you will create. Each of us is an amazing manifestor! We are constantly creating our life and worldview according to what we think about either to ourselves or say aloud to others. We are actively creating our reality, consciously as well as unconsciously. This is not the idea or creation of another; we *alone* are the creators of our reality.

Sometimes the only choice that we have in a situation is how to look at it and our attitude about it. I believe that our attitude plays a large

Dolores Fazzino

part in the creation of our reality. I have witnessed people with horrific life tragedies that have survived and thrived based on their attitudes. It really boils down to the question; "How am I going to respond to this? Will I become a victim to my circumstances or will I rise above and become empowered to do something with my life?"

Each of us is in charge of our attitude and how we show up in the world. Be grateful for all that you have in this very moment, even though it may not be where you want to be and are in a tremendous amount of emotional pain. By being grateful we create more and more in our life to be grateful for. Remember, it is focusing on what you desire that creates more of what you desire! An attitude of gratitude lays the foundation for creating the life of our dreams!

I invite you to do a Gratitude Challenge by creating a gratitude journal. Start with 150 things that you are grateful for right this very minute. Then for each of the next 30 days, write 5 things that you are grateful for. Notice any patterns or feelings that come up around these things that you are grateful for and write those down as well. By doing this exercise, you are retraining your thoughts to be filtered through your heart space. Notice how your heart soars.

Dr. Dolores Fazzino, Doctorate of Nursing Practice (DNP) is a Nurse Practitioner, a Wellness Consultant and President of *Spiritual Wellness for Life,* as well as an international featured media speaker and author.

Her Company, Spiritual Wellness for Life, bridges spirituality with physical health and wellness. She practices and trains in two worlds; the physical and the spiritual. Dolores believes that Spirituality is the glue that holds the body, mind and soul together.

With over 35 years of experience Dolores is a leading authority on combining traditional medicine, energy healing and spirituality assisting clients to move through life challenges and reconnect with the lost parts of themselves with grace and ease.

Her first book *"Spiritual Wellness for Life: Inspiring Life Stories of Forgiveness, Transformation and Healing"* is available on Amazon.com. She has a virtual practice in Encinitas, CA USA. To find out more about Dolores visit www.SpiritualWellnessForLife.com

When you show up in your life, magic happens!
~ Dolores Fazzino

Money in the Bag

Jane Cabrera

The irony is that the more you give the ego the space and freedom to express, the more access you get to hear the voice of your soul.

When it comes to money and wealth, what's your story? Are you a student of the "Law of Attraction," having some success with manifestation? Even with that success, do you still find money a struggle? You're in good company. So many adults have achieved educationally, and have been through the highs and lows of career success and job loss. Many of us have successfully raised families, owned homes, upsized and downsized as was fitting the circumstances. Yet with all of this life experience, many adults still feel a sense of powerlessness and overwhelm when it comes to money.

And it makes perfect sense. Did you know that most of your experience of money is driven by emotion, and not by intellect? And did you know that emotion is way more powerful than intellect?

I teach a weekend experiential workshop where students have an opportunity to observe their automatic thoughts, feelings and behaviors when it comes to money. The experience comes in the form of a game called "The Spending Game." Students exchange $10 for 10 "Freedom Dollars." Each game dollar is printed on 8 ½ by 11 inch bright green card stock, obviously distinguished as game money. Throughout the weekend, the students conduct transactions with each other, exchanging these dollars for goods and services within the course room setting. Information about their cash on hand and purchases are gathered throughout the weekend and are used in exercises and as a context for class discussion. In the confines of this safe classroom experience, we are able to observe behaviors that might not otherwise have been noticed.

Meet Line, a student from Norway. This was her second time through the weekend experience; so she had prepared the goods and services that she would offer in the game. She was thoroughly enjoying the experience, interacting enthusiastically with the other participants, buying and selling with a lightness and joy that just lit up the room. After several transactions, without anyone noticing, she hid her "Freedom Dollars" away in her bag.

Shawna, a student from the United States,

loves games to begin with. She approached the spending game with a sense of competitive fun, wanting to play and interact with the other participants, but also trying to figure out how to win. I noticed that after every transaction, she tucked her "Freedom Dollars" away in her bag.

This behavior is notable, because all of the other participants kept their dollars on the table in front of them, along with their workbook and other course materials. Why were these ladies hiding their play money in their bags?

Renowned psychologist Alfred Adler used the term "private logic" to describe why people do things that might not hold up to the standard of "common sense." Through his extensive work in the late 1800s and early 1900s he developed a philosophy of "Individual Psychology" that focuses on the emotional experiences and interpretations of an individual in early childhood to explain the thought and behavior habit patterns that a person exhibits in adult life. These formative experiences usually occur before the age of 7 or 8. At such a young age we don't have the power of our reasoning mind to question our impressions and conclusions, so we are imprinted with a sense of "how things are" that stays with us into our adult life, and runs below our level of awareness.

As we go about daily living in adult life, we have experiences that trigger an emotional memory from these past experiences, resulting in automatic thoughts and behaviors that don't necessarily make rational sense in the context of our life today. Using diagnostic tools that are based in the work of Alfred Adler, I help people to sort out these patterns, so that they can become aware of what is driving their behavior.

It turns out that Line from Norway, was playing the game quite successfully and she had accumulated a lot of "Freedom Dollars." Knowing how many dollars were available in the game, she was very aware that she had accumulated more money than anyone else. And she felt a bit ashamed, thinking that if the others found out, they would not want to conduct any more transactions with her. So she hid her money in her bag.

Shawna had a completely different motivation for hiding her money. Even though she was in a course room with very caring, loving people, playing a game with play "Freedom Dollars" she was consumed with a fear that someone would steal her money if she left it out in the open. So she hid her money in her bag.

Understanding a little bit about their childhood experiences, these thought and behavior patterns made perfect sense. Where Line grew up in Norway, it is considered shameful to show off that one has more than someone else. It's a complete reversal of the "Keeping Up with the Joneses" mentality that is popular here in the United States. With that early emotional conditioning, Line felt very uncomfortable displaying her dollars on the table, where others could easily see that she had more than everyone else.

Shawna on the other hand had an experience as a very young child where her brother stole her collection of coins. She was very young at the time and she loved her coins. She was very hurt that someone would take away something that she loved and she was even more hurt that it was someone close to her. The drive to avoid that kind of pain for her is automatic and with that information, it makes perfect sense why she would hide her game dollars in a room full of friends.

Knowledge of this phenomenon allowed me to provide really powerful emotional support to my Mom after my Dad passed away in 2006. My parents were married in the early '60s and despite their humble beginnings; they created financial stability and over the years multiplied that stability into a comfortable middle class lifestyle. Newly widowed, my Mom was in a position to be making financial decisions on her own for the first time in her life and was completely taken off guard by the flood of intense emotion that accompanied even simple decisions, for example, to replace a 15 year old carpet. Some of the emotion was in the ordinary course of grieving the loss of my Dad, but there was something else going on. When it came time to decide to make a purchase, she would be overwhelmed with feelings of guilt and a fear that she was spending foolishly, even though she knew intellectually that she had enough money. The intellectual awareness of having enough money made it even worse, because then she felt like she was going crazy; it didn't make any sense. Engulfed in the experience of all of that intense emotion, and self-judgment, my Mom would call me to, in her words "talk her off the ledge."

Here's the advice I would give my Mom.

1. You feel what you feel.

Feelings are just a response to a stimulus, and provide very useful information. It doesn't have to make sense to you or to anyone else. So the first thing to accept is that you feel what you feel, it's your experience and you have every right to feel it.

2. Slow down, pay attention and just notice.

Think of yourself like a scientist doing research, and all you are doing is gathering data. Slow down, pay attention and just observe. Don't judge what you are observing and don't try to change it. What do you feel? Are there any sensations in the body that you notice, perhaps a slight headache or tightness in the chest? Just notice those things. What emotions are you feeling? And really pay attention to notice all of them. It is common to experience two or more streams of emotion at the same time, for example the excitement and positive expectation of finding a carpet you love, exists simultaneously with the guilt and fear of spending foolishly.

The most important part here is to just notice as much detail as possible. To be sure you capture and remember the emotion, its best if you can write it down. You do not need to do anything to change your feelings or behavior, just notice it and become aware of it.

3. Get some sleep.

The act of observing yourself and your emotions is the first step in the process of transformation. Just like a caterpillar that will transform into a butterfly, there is a time to cocoon, and just allow the transformation to happen. For humans, the consolidation of new neural pathways in the brain takes place during sleep and by observing your automatic behaviors and emotions, you are giving your brain lots of new stimulus to work with and you naturally open yourself to new insights and new possibilities, without having to force anything.

There is so much information out there about reprogramming the brain and how to take steps to change a habit. Forget about all of that, at least for now. Awareness does so much naturally. Just give yourself time to observe, notice, accept yourself the way you are and sleep.

My Mom recently reflected on being a child growing up in the '40s, the post-depression years. Other kids had things like bicycles and dancing lessons; she wanted those things too. She was disappointed and hurt when she was told that she couldn't have those things, and that her family could not afford to spend money foolishly. At that young tender age, she interpreted that to mean that she didn't deserve to have the things that she wanted. Those unhealed emotions came flooding back suddenly when as an adult; she had the opportunity to give herself the things that she wanted. That feeling of going crazy wasn't crazy at all; in fact, it makes perfect sense in the light of her early emotional experience.

The processing and healing of these emotions is an ongoing journey. Even with the awareness and perspective of where the emotions are coming from, the automatic emotional reaction still occurs when she makes financial decisions; my Mom says that she has to "talk to herself" to process through it. The emotions today are less intense, she moves through it much faster and she enjoys a level of confidence in her purchasing decisions as never before.

Shawna was thrilled that in the days and weeks following the learning that occurred in her weekend course that she didn't have to do anything! The urge to protect and hide her possessions is still present, and she is enjoying a new sense of freedom in being able to observe those feelings, rather than by being driven by them.

Line made a public display of her abundance when she and her husband recently invested in a camper so that they could enjoy outdoor excursions with their young children. Line expressed that she always wanted a camper and thought of it as a future thing. She had the epiphany of "why not now?" after shifting her perspective in the weekend course. Although the decision prompted a critical response from family and friends ("How can you spend so foolishly?") Line experienced a sense of freedom in not being moved or concerned so much with the opinions of others. She and her family are experiencing the joy of a powerful decision to enjoy their abundance in the here and now, that's what matters most.

I invite you to explore your own emotions and habits around money. Join me for an experiential weekend. For more information, please go to MoneyandLifeFreedom.com.

Jane Cabrera started her career as a CPA and has over 20 years of experience as a corporate controller, specializing in organizational change management. She is an expert in internal controls, business process implementation, and corporate oversight.

Through her experiences with leading organizational change, Jane became increasingly aware of how human behavioral dynamics impacted the progress of any and all business initiatives.

Following her passions and personal initiative in 2007, Jane delved deeper into the study of human behavior and human energy dynamics. This led her to study and experience leading edge technology for adult learning. Jane holds several certifications and has written and taught workshops that guide others to create permanent shifts towards their life goals.

Through her workshops and mentoring, Jane has helped individuals, families and businesses to use simple, practical tools that create dramatic desirable results.

MoneyandLifeFreedom.com

Regardless of your circumstances, environment, history or public opinion, you can create the life you want to live.
~ Karen Fogerty

This Is Your Magic!

Karin Fogerty

Regardless of your circumstances, environment, history or public opinion, you can create the life you want to live.

It was Sunday morning. I was two hours into a marathon church service, writhing quietly in excruciating pain. Resisting every moment of my sentence on the hard wooden pew, instead of listening to the sermon, I was mentally blaming the organizers of this whole event for torturing us. I hadn't been raised with any structured religion, so this was not in my wheelhouse.

Having grown up with the ability to "hear" energy in addition to audible sound, it was common for me—even as a young child—to experience an overwhelming amount of sensory input on a daily basis. I could hear weird things like electricity flowing through wires, sound coming through outdoor telephone lines, and songs that people were thinking of in their heads. I was also able to see colors swirling around people, which I found out were called auras. My sensitivity to energy was so strong that I could feel the emotions of other people, even if they were on the other side of a wall!

Unfortunately, these extraordinary abilities hadn't helped me personally one bit. Years of physical ailments, migraines and skin disorders had created a mounting chronic depression. Instead of awarding me superpowers, my sensitivities compounded the pain I was entrenched in. It felt like these abilities themselves were burying me.

That day in church, I was freshly divorced and bitter enough to claw anything that moved my way. I dressed only in black and brown and wore my hair spiked. I looked a fright. As a young woman in my twenties, cultivating a repellant presence was the best defense I could conjure up to isolate myself. If anyone directed one more speck of attention, demand, or judgment my way, I would surely explode and the desperation I held inside of me would spray these holy walls black and brown.

Even pain killers, a hospitalization and a litany of counselors had been unable to lighten my load of sadness. I was sick of the fake smile I wore for my family and friends. I was lost, and today's event was essentially my last stop. I was out of hope.

My friend had looped me into joining her for the morning at church to see a man. He was supposed to be some big cheese in the spiritual world. But quite frankly, as I impatiently observed him sitting on stage during the service I thought, *Big deal. So he can sit in silent meditation for close to three hours now. What's so great about that? I'm done. I'm out of here.* So off to the reception room I flew to grab some free food on my exit. No sense in this being a complete waste of my time, right?

A plate in hand, shoveling up brownies as fast as I could, it happened. I saw the same man again, across the room. The service must have finally been put to rest. From my vantage point, as I stared at this so called pooh-bah, it oddly appeared as if he were standing inside a giant gold bubble. I squeezed my eyes shut really tight and then re-opened them to the size of golf balls to confirm I wasn't hallucinating. As the room silently reappeared in front of me, I saw the man was not only still encased in what appeared to be a gold bubble, but he was walking himself and his gold bubble right toward me! I slowly realized that what I saw as a gold bubble was his aura. It startled me. I had never seen a gold aura before.

When the man got about six feet from me, he tipped his head in acknowledgment of my bugged eyes, smiled and then passed by me as my mouth dropped to whisk the floor. I continued to stare in awe. This man was a human light bulb. So much light was coming through his body; it looked translucent; like his cells had been individually scrubbed to a sparkle. My world hiccupped and I took notice.

"Whatever he has, I want that!" became my new mantra. For the first time since my childhood, I had witnessed the sunshine that I, too, used to have in my body, which had long ago dimmed. It was the single greatest reminder I have ever experienced.

How could I possibly get my state of gold back? How could I recover the part of me that sang and rejoiced in the freedom to play? I didn't have an answer that day, but I vowed to figure it out; I would find out what walking in gold felt like again.

This decision, almost a childlike curiosity to uncover the secrets of a human light bulb became a dedicated thirty-year exploration and career.

I began taking classes on spiritual energy from the man in the gold bubble. From him, I learned to view my sensitivities as an asset, rather than a liability. Whereas I had turned into a virtual sponge of pain, I found out that all I needed was an exit door for all the extraneous "stuff" I didn't want in my world; stuff like the energy of other people's disappointments, criticisms and even their problems! I had absorbed all of this into my personal space.

So the first thing I learned was how to release what I had been holding onto. It felt so incredible to lose this heaviness I had carried for years—which didn't even belong to me in the first place!

My sadness lessened. My migraines became fewer. I no longer thought I was going crazy. I now realized that I had just been missing some important instructions, like being issued a car with no driver's manual. No one had ever taught me about my soul energy! What I was finding was that this "soul energy" thing was a critical part of my life that shaped my moods, fueled my creativity, supported my drive and could even heal my body. I was empowered with my new knowledge.

The answer to the question I had challenged myself to find was simple; learn the mechanics of my energetic body so I could keep it healthy. It would then teach the rest of me how to stay healthy in body, mind and spirit. When all of me was in balance, the clear energy appeared to me as gold.

I was so inspired by every nugget I was learning that I developed my intuitive abilities into a level of expertise that I found could help others! I refined my ability to hear energy to the point where I could deliberately tap into people's subconscious thoughts. This allowed me to give them communication on what was hindering their personal growth or causing them pain.

Then I decided to take things a step further: If correcting the mechanics of my own energy could revolutionize my life, wouldn't teaching people around me how to recognize "their light" benefit them too? I began teaching my clients techniques on how to use their own gifts to release pain and energy.

One day, I was asked to officiate a wedding. I was so honored. Since that day of the church service I had despised so much, the shift in my own spiritual path had actually led me to become a licensed minister. Fittingly, as I performed the service, I experienced being in my own gold bubble for the first time. It was magic.

Building a spiritual business so that I can share my skills with others, I've been blessed to have helped over 15,000 people learn more about their own energy, how to get out of pain and how to create happy lives. I founded a spiritual center in Southern California where I developed master healing programs so that my students could join me in elevating themselves and others emotionally, mentally and energetically.

Providing spiritual communication, energy healings, and instructional guidance on people's soul energy has given back to me exponentially. These personal interactions have taught me countless lessons and brought immeasurable love and joy into my life. I've learned to appreciate my gifts and have discovered that a shiny jewel of spiritual wisdom waits on the other side of every challenge.

Although I use and teach a wide array of techniques for managing energy, my philosophy for having an enhanced partnership with yourself is actually simple. *This is your magic!*

Love Yourself

The best gift you can give yourself is that of your own friendship.

With all of the challenges, opportunities and unexpected changes that happen during a lifetime, learn to be your own champion. If you're not treating yourself with the same love and respect that you would extend to your loved ones, how can you expect to enjoy this body and life that you created for yourself? Waiting for a partner, parent or friend to provide you with the nurturing your innermost sanctum desires means you could be waiting for a very long time. So establish a solid relationship with the one person you will always be able to count on: You.

A great way to bring some love into your world is to treat yourself with a little something special every day: a favorite song, a walk in the park, a healthy meal, a sumptuous bath or even a compliment. Anything that nourishes your body, mind and soul will reinforce self-love and nurture a happy heart.

Trust Yourself

A creative genius resides in every one of us.

Call it your gut, call it intuition—this is your higher wisdom trying to tell you a truth that you may be overlooking. You were born with your own brilliant ingenuity and it still resides inside and around you energetically. This is your spiritual intelligence. You may remember what it was like to use this intuitive resource in your early childhood, when permission for freedom and wonder was more prevalent.

It's never too late to reclaim what is yours! Try to bring as much of your spiritual intelligence into your body as possible. A quick and easy way to start is to imagine bringing a golden sun in through the top of your head and visualize it filling up every cell of your body. This simple act not only shifts your overall energy to a higher state but it brings in more of your own natural intelligence and information, which resides just above your head.

Forgive Yourself

Forgiveness is the gateway to freedom.

Think of all the hours you have stacked up in your life blaming yourself for one thing or another. Has brow-beating ever brought you an answer to your questions, a solution to your problems or relief from your emotional turmoil? The blame game is a dead-end road. Whether you are blaming another or smackin' yourself around silly, it's all "stop" energy! That means that you will remain immobilized in that area of your life until you let go of your judgment.

Give yourself permission to have a good cry or a good physical release and then *let yourself off the hook* from the criticisms you are holding against yourself. Remind yourself that whatever it was, you made the best decision you could based on what you knew at that time. We must move on to live another day if we want to enjoy the divine graces we intended to have as children.

Self-punishment only serves those who have judged us. At the end of the day there is no golden reward for suffering. Here's a little secret: the energy of forgiveness vibrates at a gold color. Imagine bringing in a gold sun that is filled with forgiveness and feed yourself with acceptance.

To know yourself, mind, body and spirit, is to

operate at your highest potential. Knowing oneself does not happen overnight but the state of heightened spiritual and physical productivity is available to each and every one of us. This knowledge doesn't require any special prerequisites, isn't selective about who can benefit from it and can be easily learned.

If you would like to know more about your own spiritual energy, I'm excited to offer you a free copy of my e-book, "7 Secrets to Unleashing Your Ultimate Potential" at

www.UnleashYourUltimatePotential.com.

You *can* create the life you want to live!

Karin Fogerty recognized her own ability to hear energy as a child; she grew up expanding her extraordinary sensitivities to seeing, hearing and feeling energy. These gifts were accelerated during her teens and twenties with formal instruction on developing her clairaudience and clairvoyance and then her instructional skills to help promote others' gifts of insight.

Karin is a master energy healer, spiritual teacher, licensed minister and the founder and director of three spiritual centers in Los Angeles. She has performed over 15,000 case studies during her professional career, helping individuals break through their barriers to become their highest and most creative selves.

Karin has always followed her own heart, passionately expressing her creativity, through writing; designing clothes and jewelry; graphic design and performing arts.

A Southern California resident, Karin is thrilled to offer her intuitive gifts of communication online to help people across the globe via Unleash Your Ultimate Potential.

www.UnleashYourUltimatePotential.com

How to Rebuild and Refocus Your Business for Lasting Success

Linda Coleman-Willis

I made lots of mistakes so you don't have to.

I can save you the time, effort and frustration of making the same mistakes I made. I decided to share my story here in hopes of also saving you some of the heartaches and pain of financial loss that I experienced. I don't regret leaving my corporate job in the financial industry in 1996 and establishing a speaking and training business in the field of Personal Growth and Development.

I learned great lessons during the years of ups and downs that followed. I certainly am grateful for the level of success I was able to achieve. By 2001 my dream of a successful business had come true. I had major contracts with Fortune 500 companies, government agencies and organizations across the country.

On September 11, 2001 (9/11), it all came crashing down with the announcement that an airplane had hit the World Trade Center in New

York City and the Pentagon in Washington, D.C. The contracts were gone and my business was in jeopardy. Companies no longer wanted to assume the risk of flying their key executives or me across the country. In a flash, my industry had changed forever.

In response, I put my nose to the grindstone, determined to regain the business success I had spent years building. Working hard had always worked for me and this time was no different. Within a few months I landed two long-term training contracts and was on my way back to profitability. A few years later I landed another lucrative contract and was back to the level of success I had achieved prior to 9/11.

This time, it was an accident that took me out of my business for almost two years. It was painful to watch everything I had worked for begin to erode once again. I had to take a good hard look at how I was *doing* my business. I was a solopreneur (an entrepreneur who worked alone, "solo"). I delivered the keynotes, did the training programs, wrote and published the books, wrote a monthly column which was published in several news publications, hosted a radio and a TV talk show, and was the "go-to" business expert on NBC's *MAKING IT! Minority Success Stories*. I had a personal assistant, a data-entry person and an occasional contractor for hire, but the full responsibility for the running of my business was squarely on my shoulder. A shoulder that now needed major surgery and a long rehabilitation process. *Who is minding the business now?*

I was the product and the talent and I built a great CAREER, but I did NOT build a business. I found myself once again embarking on the road to rebuilding and this time with a renewed commitment to get it right. If 9/11 or an accident were to happen today, would your business survive or would you have to start from the beginning?

Every entrepreneur/business person needs a consultant/mentor, role-model or coach. The fastest way to learn any business is to study someone who has been successful at it. This person has already paid the price to learn what you need to know. Whether it is "what to do" or "what not to do," you'll want to absorb all the information you can while you are working with that person. Hire people to do what they are experts at, so that you can do only what YOU are an EXPERT at to help you grow and expand your business and your skills. When your business is not growing, it is not just standing still, it is dying.

This didn't really become evident to me until I was injured and all the cracks in my business structure began to show up. I then made the decision to hire a consultant and adopt the strategies she designed for my business. I discovered that when I got reliable, measurable feedback, I was able to make intelligent, informed decisions that led to real, concrete and lasting results.

If you are a soloprenuer and you are feeling like you have to do it all yourself, you don't. In fact, you can't and when you try, you miss out on more opportunities than you can ever imagine. When you can approach a situation with fresh eyes, you are no longer defined by past fears and failures and you can make informed decisions.

As a business development consultant, I have found that most successful people work hard, but all hit plateaus and have blind spots. Many have entire areas of potential that they have never explored or pursued.

One of my clients, the Owner/CEO of an Information Technology Company, has contracts with several Fortune 500 companies. He is so busy working; he sometimes doesn't keep up with what his clients' changing needs are. We helped him design a process for his customers to share their needs with him; it allows him to address those needs and create new IT systems, which in turn results in more business for his company.

Other clients are focused and motivated, but most don't make time for strategic thinking about their business. I have a client that was spending thousands of dollars a month on advertising, but zero dollars on training and development for his employees, therefore costing him customers. We customized an employee train-the-trainer program so he would have in-house trainers to train new and current employees. The result was that he never had untrained employees handling customers. His business increased 20% in 90 days and still continues to improve.

Over the years, I've met many business people who desperately want to be successful but who are unwilling to invest in themselves or their business. They think they can learn everything they need to know on their own at the exact time they need to know it. You probably can eventually learn on your own, but if you can avoid making some very costly mistakes or cut the time it takes to learn on your own in half, would you agree it is worth it to engage an expert?

You are obviously not one of those people who think they can do everything on their own because you are reading this book. I realize this is the digital age and we are all heavily dependent on technology; however there are some basic business rules for building or rebuilding your business for lasting success:

1. Know Your Outcome – Own Your Vision

Many business people are too vague here. I

certainly was. To create a successful business, you need to ask some hard questions. *What is it that I want to happen here? What outcome do I want to achieve? What end result do I want?* Your responses to these questions will determine how things will eventually turn out. Defining and owning your vision is the first step in goal-setting. A vision is a clear, distinctive and specific view of the future that allows you to set goals, make plans and solve problems that will guide your business. A clear vision will help you see unlimited choices and possibilities; you see what can be instead of what is.

2. Expand Your Awareness – Exceed Your Reach

The key to expanded awareness is letting go of the old. It requires us to move outside our comfort zones and familiar boundaries. Notice whether or not what you are doing is working. Don't hold on to something that is not working because you have invested time or money. It may have worked in the past but it is not working now. Past successes can sometimes hinder present and future success. It was difficult for me to let go of ideas, techniques and strategies that had proven successful in my business, but were no longer getting the results I needed in today's world. I had to persist through and ask the hard question: *Am I getting the results I want?* In order to make intelligent, informed decisions, we need reliable, measurable feedback. By evaluating our progress, we know where we may need to redirect our focus and energy.

3. **Exercise Flexibility – Embrace Change**

Don't avoid opportunity because it was not in the original plan. Be open to looking at things from a different perspective, to see things differently than you have in the past, in order to DO something different. Continue to change until you get results. We can change what we think, our perception, by reinterpreting and redefining what something means to us. We can also change our procedures, by changing what we do and how we do it. This empowers us to expand and grow personally and professionally and provide great benefits to our business success. Although change entails uncertainty, it can also bring unlimited opportunity. To embrace change, look for the catalyst for change in your industry (computers, information, technology, etc.) and learn the best way to utilize it in your business. Part of your business strategy should be to anticipate and continually initiate change to maintain leadership in your field.

4. Be Decisive – Make Smart Choices

Business success is determined by the choices we make and the actions we take. It can oftentimes feel overwhelming, especially when we face many options and unknown consequences. However, success is not some distant external goal. Success comes from making tough decisions and dynamic choices that are not bound by old habits and beliefs. To grow and improve in business, as in life, we are required to go beyond our present knowledge and experience to move outside our comfort zones and current boundaries, into unfamiliar territories and to explore new opportunities. This means being open to new ideas, approaches and practices, then having the willingness and courage to try them out. Success comes from all directions. We have to remain open to receiving. We must evaluate what is working and we also have to look at and evaluate what is NOT working. Some tough questions are: *What choices/actions did I make that moved me forward? Which ones got in the way?* Our business is shaped by the decisions we make in every minute.

5. You Can Build a Successful Business

Be constantly learning about your business, your industry, your customers and about your own mistakes. You don't need to learn everything at once; learn what you need to remain competitive in your area of expertise. To build and maintain a successful business you need to:
a. Keep current clients.
b. Get new clients.
c. Develop and improve products and/or services.
d. Build a successful infrastructure.
e. Find experts that can help.

Whether you are just beginning your business or are rebuilding and refocusing, know that things are always changing. The market is changing, your area of work is morphing as technology is changing on a daily basis. There will be the need to hire others who are experts in their fields so that you can continue to be the focused expert in yours. Be open to learning, growing and changing as your industry does and success is yours for the taking.

Linda Coleman-Willis is the Business Development Specialist, recognized as an expert in her field. She is an author, professional speaker, corporate trainer and successful entrepreneur who has guided numerous companies and individuals to achieve outstanding results.

Linda is the founder of *Business Development for Success*, an organization that helps corporate leaders, business owners and entrepreneurs develop more effective business strategies. She provides her clients with on-going support to stay focused on solutions, push through challenges and achieve new levels of success.

The results to her clients are satisfied

customers, increased profits and explosive growth! Her messages of overcoming obstacles and getting results have created positive changes for thousands individuals and businesses nationwide.

Let us show you how to apply KEY business concepts, strategies, and systems that will set your business apart and create lasting success.

Take the Business Development for Success
Personalized Business Consultation Analysis
Visit <u>www.businessdevelopmentforsuccess.com</u>

Excellence

Tom Antion

The only way to exceed the average income in your field is to become better known.

"Excellence" is the word. This is how it worked for me anyway. I really didn't plan to be where I am today. The two most recent phases of my business life were pretty much thrust upon me because of my quest for excellence.

Let me explain.

My father who came from the "old country" in the early 1900's, and ended up with a 2nd grade education, brought me up believing that I could be whatever I wanted to be if I was willing to work for it . . . and become excellent. I lived by this principle my entire adult life, even when I was a paid practical joker.

After six grueling years in the nightclub business, I decided that whatever I got into next was going to be fun for me and fun for my customers. This was a stark contrast to the miserable nightclub business that looked like fun on the surface, but was largely comprised of people drowning their sorrows, fighting and acting like idiots while my employees and I ducked flying beer bottles and bullets....Yes I said "bullets."

Prankmasters was born.

For six years in the Washington, D.C. area I was the king of practical jokes for pay. This was long before the more modern "Punked", "Jackass" and the various other practical joke shows that have emerged. My only predecessor and inspiration was "Candid Camera."

During the prank years I always thought there was something bigger out there for me. I had no idea what it was; maybe a TV show or maybe a movie. I didn't know what it was, but I knew it was out there looking for me.

One day I was in the now defunct "Crown Books" in Greenbelt, MD and my head literally bumped a book by Dottie Walters called "*Speak and Grow Rich*." I ate this book up in one day. Then I called Dottie and paid for a consultation. That day a professional speaking career was born.

Now what?

I was funny from having written and delivered

over 1000 comic performances over the past six years. I had lots of business experience renting apartments, running a nightclub and running various other businesses, but I had no idea how to craft a speech for businesspeople in a hotel meeting room. I didn't know about meeting planners, microphones, storytelling and such. Heck, I'd been pretty much a comic buffoon for a long, long time.

With my dad's teaching ringing in my ear I set out to be an "excellent" professional speaker. I joined the local chapter of the National Speakers Association. I took over the librarianship so I had access to hundreds of hours of other speakers telling how they wowed their audiences. I started buying every book I could and now have a library of over 200 books on public speaking. I've read each one cover to cover and many of them I've read multiple times.

When I broke into speaking, the elders of the speaker's organization told me I was better than people charging five times as much. I'm not tooting my own horn here, but I got so good that people started begging me to teach them how to be better. When other pro speakers start asking you to teach them, I guess you could say that was at least some evidence I was pretty darn good.

So here's what happened...

I was spending so much time helping other speakers I couldn't find the time to get my own work done. That's when I started creating training materials for speakers, and when my classic (if I do say so myself) "Wake 'em Up" book was born. (Did you notice a lot of things are getting "born" in this essay ☺.)

In my quest to become an "excellent" professional speaker, people started to notice and they were asking for my help. This led me to be a very expensive public speaking and sales presentation expert for several years, during which time; I was able to develop a complete line of speaker products, a blog and the largest email list of professional speakers in the world. When I transitioned to the next phase of my business life I was charging $20,000.00 per day for my work.

The Commercial Web

The Internet was around long before you could sell stuff on it. Circa 1994 the commercial World Wide Web came along. Believe me...it called to me. It said, "Tom, it's hard enough to sell your products across the street. How would you like to sell them around the world from your desktop?"

I was sooooooo in! My dad's voice was more than ringing in my ear. It was like my head was stuck in the Liberty Bell. I dove in with both feet. I read every possible book (there weren't that many at the time) on how to sell online. I scratched and clawed and tried everything there was to try. I learned a lot but didn't make a nickel for the first two years.

Then I ran across Corey Rudl. He was the 28 year old "grandfather" of Internet marketing making millions a year from his apartment. Just like before with Dottie Walters, I bought his course and a consultation (Yikes! $1200.00 for half an hour) but it was worth it. Just one of the tips he taught me, has been worth over a million dollars over the years.

Multi-Millionaire Status

Only four short years after meeting with Corey, implementing what he taught me and continuing to learn, I hit multi-millionaire status. How did I do that? Well, here we go again. In my efforts to be "excellent" at Internet marketing, just to sell my own stuff, people started to notice. Just like before they started asking me for help where it got to the point I couldn't get my own work done. That's when I founded "ButtCamp"... a goofy name for a very serious Internet marketing seminar.

I should take a moment to explain "ButtCamp." Coming from the comic background I had, I was not about to name my seminar "Bootcamp" like everyone else names theirs. When I was pondering an appropriate name for the seminar, I thought to myself, "I'm sitting here on my butt in front of this computer making money; I ought to call the seminar 'ButtCamp'." It's the longest running Internet marketing seminar I know of. I've done them in 12 countries around the world, but in England they made me call it "Bum Camp" hahaha.

Besides selling products online I had ButtCamp and I started one of the longest running most successful mentor programs for Internet marketing, which I still run to this day.

The bottom line is when you strive for and become excellent, people will notice and ask you to teach them what you know.

Here Are a Few Tips:

As part of this essay I was asked to give you, the reader, three tips in my field of expertise. Since my two main fields, professional speaking and Internet marketing aren't really the same, I figured I would "excellently" give you tips on both.

Professional Speaking Tips

- Attempt to give the audience more immediately usable tips than any speaker they have ever heard. You will always be in demand.

- Thoroughly prepare for every speaking engagement by knowing your audience, preparing comments that apply specifically to them and choosing humor appropriate for the occasion.

- Arrive early to get all your equipment and notes set so you can spend time just before the meeting interacting with the audience members. Stay late and be there for them. Don't roll in and out like a Diva.

Internet Marketing Tips

- Know the keywords people would type in to Google when looking for your type of product or service. You will use these keywords in all phases of your business.

- Treat your online business like a business. So many people fail because they think they will be on the beach all day sipping Mint Julips with money pouring in to their checking account. Yes it can happen, but only after lots of hard work building the business.

- Study Internet marketing like a fiend. The

more you know, the less you will spend on your business and the more profitable you will be faster.

To recap:

I did everything possible to be an excellent speaker and it paid off with millions of dollars of speaking fees and millions of dollars in speaker training products sold. Then I did everything possible to be excellent on the Internet and in only four years I became a multimillionaire and for over 21 years now I've been making millions of dollars per year selling my stuff and training others to do so. I hope you're getting the point here. Always do what it takes to be "excellent" and you could reap rewards far bigger than you ever imagined. I can't wait to hear about your successes.

Tom Antion is an Internet Multi-Millionaire. He has been the founder of several one-of-a-kind businesses including "The Great Internet Marketing Retreat Center" where people come in from all over the world to study Internet marketing in the lap of luxury and "The Internet Marketing Training Center of Virginia" the only licensed and dedicated distance learning Internet marketing school in the country.

Tom also has the largest opt in email list of professional speakers:

http://www.GreatSpeaking.com with 100,000 subscribers in 80 countries, the longest running public speaking blog and the longest running speaker shop.

http://www.GreatPublicSpeaking.BlogSpot.com

http://www.Antion.com/speakershop.htm

Tom is also a consumer advocate and has a TV show in development.

http://www.ScamBrigade.com

You can reach Tom at his office 757-431-1366 or through http://www.Antion.com

Time Management
Don't Make Your Deadline
a Dreadline

Nellie Williams

The truth is, no one can manage time. You can only manage yourself and what you do with your time.

Tick, tock. Can you hear it? No. Silently, time marches on. The buzzer sounds on the alarm clock. Time to get up. The buzzer sounds on the game show. Do you have the winning answer? The buzzer sounds at the end of shift. Time to go home. Did you finish your assignment?

Even Cinderella knew the importance of 12 o'clock midnight! Her gilded coach would turn back into a pumpkin. Her handsome white horses would turn back into mice. Her gorgeous gown would return to tatters. She lost a glass slipper running from the Prince she had just fallen in love with, for the sake of time.

Every American knows the deadline of April 15th. Some stretch that deadline out as far as

October 15th when we request an extension of time to file our tax returns. Filing that extension does not, however, eliminate the requirement to file. It just gives us more time.

During tax season I might be seen as a workaholic. The truth is, every one of my clients is my boss. Some bosses I please more than others. Some bosses I please more completely than others. Even though there is only one April 15th every year, I have multiple clients who I work with to meet their deadlines.

In my business, time is of the essence. My big midnight is on April 15th. But I have a lot of other deadlines leading up to April 15th. Perhaps some of the tools I use can help you in your life, too.

How do you feel when you finish something on time? You feel good, accomplished, satisfied and deserving. How do you feel when you miss the deadline? It can be very damaging and stressful. What is the consequence to you? With the IRS, it is late fees and penalties. What is the impact on other people? Potentially a cranky friend or boss, depending on what your relationship is with that person. Sometimes we miss the deadline deliberately. That's not such a great idea with the IRS, but in other areas, it's a fact that this happens. When Congress does this, temporary tax laws expire. Don't you just love it? The catching up can be a costly nightmare.

Every day is unique. Every tax season is unique. For me, this year was the year of technology. Not just technology, but technology failure. Just like people have an expected lifetime, machines have an expected useful life. Just like with people, there is often no warning signal that time's up.

This year was computer server failure time. March 15th! There is never a good time for an emergency. But only April 10th would have been worse. How do you handle an interruption? Here are a few tips that will help YOU manage things when things go wrong.

TIP ONE: Have a Contingency Plan

Here is where I needed a Plan B, a contingency plan. I learned that my first contingency plan as a little girl. My father, a volunteer fireman, drilled us on what to do in case our house was on fire. 1. Get out of the house. 2. Go across the street to a designated meeting place. 3. Call the fire department. Even today my husband and I have an "in case of fire" contingency plan.

When I realized on Sunday my computer server was down, I realized I did have a contingency plan. I used my cell phone to text my trusted, reliable computer technician. Patrick, my computer "doctor", said he'd be at my office first thing Monday to take a look. He took my server to his "high-tech hospital" to see if the server would be repaired or replaced. He would let me know....

Patrick called the next day with good news and bad news. The good news was that all of my treasured client data and all of my various software programs were totally safe and intact. The bad news was that my server was beyond repair. Like it is for any living thing, there is often no advance warning of impending disaster. I needed a new computer server. FAST!

We talked about my options and choices. Once I made my decision, Patrick said he'd have my new server ready to install by the end of the week. I still had my desktop computer. He made sure I could access the internet and do my emailing. I was limping along but my tax business would be on hold until the 21st of March.

Thank goodness, all the precious, sensitive, confidential client data was secure. But not being able to access my crashed computer server was like having a race car at the gate; full of fuel, engine running, but with some secret parking brake keeping the car from moving forward. Who would get the blue ribbon, the gold cup, the million dollar prize?

I would still keep the clients' appointments as scheduled. I just needed to develop a new temporary system for preparing their returns in stages. April 15th was only a few weeks away. I was not comfortable with putting all these clients on extension.

In the early years of my business, a colleague shared this belief: "Every single day for a tax return preparer is equal to one week in any other line of work." As a business owner, I set my own hours but seem to work about 90 hours a week during tax season.

If your business is a corporation, you know the importance of March 15th; the date corporate income tax returns are due. If you cannot file your business return by March 15th, you must request an extension of time to file. If you file late without an extension, you are just late.

Was your mother like my mother? Did she tell you, "Never put off until tomorrow that which you can do today."? I am so glad my normal practice is to file those corporate extensions early.

Your personal return is due April 15th. If you do not file on time or if you file later under extension, you could be a tax delinquent. One of my clients is so uncomfortable dealing with his taxes that he files an extension every year. The anxiety he exhibits is so unnecessary. He always has enough income tax withheld from his paycheck to generate a tax refund due him. He dreads taxes so much he makes his tax deadline a *dreadline.*

The end results rarely change by waiting. You've just had more time to worry. You think you are putting it out of your mind. But as long as your task is unfinished, the thought is still there. It is an "attention unit" renting space in your subconscious mind.

TIP TWO: Identify your commitments.

What must you do? When must you do it? Do you over-commit? Do you try to cram too much to do in too little time? I confess. I have been guilty of that. I think we all have at one time or another. We deserve to be kinder to ourselves AND to the people we are serving.

I rely on my daily calendar. It holds all appointments, both business and personal. As long as I put the right information on the right date at the right time, all is well. Before the computer, the calendar was on paper. Some people still like some of the paper planners available.

In addition to filing cabinets for client documents, I have an accordion file at my desk which has a section for every month of the year. This is where I store papers I don't need today, but I will need later, like airline itinerary, boarding pass, hotel confirmation, event registration, etc., for trips. Future bills due and software renewal reminders are there too.

Whatever you are looking for, you will find it in the last place you look. Some things get filed away. Other things are kept on the desk or on the bookshelf where I can see them. For me, out of sight is often out of mind. I don't want to miss a deadline because a task is not staring me in the face.

What makes us able to meet the challenges we put in front of us? Just one more. I can do just one more. Does the deadline motivate you to action? Are you deadline driven?

TIME is the great equalizer. Every single person on this planet is given 24 hours every day. We cannot stop the sun from rising. We cannot stop the sun from setting. Another day is done. In life we sometimes have "do-overs", but we cannot get this day, this 24 hours back. We can save time, but we cannot bank time. Once it is spent, it is gone.

Have you ever missed an important event? Did it sneak up on you? Deadlines can be a mixed bag bringing both happiness and heartache. Many of our life's events involve an investment of money in addition to an investment of time. The birth of a child, a graduation from school, a wedding, a divorce and a funeral are all life events that usually involve a gift of money or a gift that costs money. The best gift you can bring to these events is the time you take to be there. Manage your time to be able to be a gift to others.

Time can be a date on the calendar or an hour on the clock. Time marches on. We cannot turn back the clock. We can plan in advance. We can be the victor instead of the victim of time.

TIP THREE: Know your internal clock.

Are you a morning glory? Are you a night owl? When during the day are you the most productive? Do you find yourself lagging at the same time each day? That clearly is not your most productive time. Can you identify your power hour, the time you are most productive?

We have so many digital aids these days. I use the alarm feature on my cell phone to alert me. I use the note pad on my cell phone for important to-do notes. You may use internet based tools that make it easy to check your schedules from wherever you are.

What kind of time management do you practice?

Is it "just-in-time" management?

Is it "in-the-nick-of-time" management?

I encourage you to put some of these tips to

160

work in your life so that time doesn't run away from you.

As busy as we make our lives, remember this: "Enjoy life! This is not a dress rehearsal."

Nellie Williams, EA, is a former IRS Tax Audit Supervisor from Phoenix, Arizona. Between her many years with the IRS and over 30 years in her own tax business, Nellie has personally examined and prepared more than 20,000 individual and small business tax returns. She has also represented hundreds of other preparers' clients being audited by the IRS. Having been named Exemplary ERO (Electronic Return Originator) by her former employer, the IRS, Nellie, also being an expert in time management is a supporter of electronic filing of tax returns.

Ms. Williams, aka *The IRS Insider*, enjoys helping you learn the rules of the tax game so you can play to win. She is the founder of Bullet ProofYourTaxes.com, her signature system AuditProofYourTaxes.com and creator of the eye-opening, time and tax-saving coaching program *Keep the IRS off Your Back and Out of Your Pocket.* ©™

www.auditproofyourtaxes.com

"The truth is, no one can manage time. You can only manage yourself and what you do with your time."
~ Nellie Williams

Afformations®: The Missing Piece to Your Abundant Lifestyle Business

Noah St. John

A true mentor believes in you before you believe in yourself.

Have you ever gone zip lining?

Zip lining is an adventure sport where you strap yourself into a harness and go zooming through the air suspended on a steel cable. If you've never done it, have you ever wanted to try it? Or, maybe you're thinking, "I would NEVER go zip lining!"

Well, the truth is that I'm a nerd and a bookworm. My idea of an exciting day is to go to the library. My wife, however, is an adventure junkie – so of course we match perfectly!

When my wife and I were planning our honeymoon, she said, "Let's go zip lining!" And I'm thinking, "How can I get out of this?" But I didn't want to look like a wimp to my bride-to-be, so I (gulp) agreed.

On our honeymoon, I find myself on the Caribbean island of St. Kitts, getting ready to go zip lining for the first time. Three big, burly men serve as our group guides, and they drive us in a truck up a mountain on this windy dirt road. We go up, up, up for what seems like miles. Then our group piles out of the truck and climb up a set of wooden stairs to a small platform high up on the mountaintop.

One of the big guides' straps on his gear, hooks onto the zip line, turns and says, "See you on the other side!" And zzzzzzzzzzzzzzzzip! Off he goes into infinity.

Then one of the other guides, who is standing there on the platform with the rest of us tourists, turns to me and says, "Okay, you're first."

Me??, I'm thinking. *Why do I have to go first?*

But again, I don't want to look scared in front of my new bride (even though I'm terrified), so I walk over to the edge of the platform and look down.

And my brain says to me, *we are definitely going to die!*

So I have a moment to decide what I'm going to do.

I could back down and say I'm not going. That means I would have to walk back miles down that dirt road, because the truck has now gone. So that's out of the question.

Another option is to just stay on the platform and not move. But then how will I get down? And how will I face my new bride after wimping out?

Finally, I review my other and only realistic option – which is to go forward.

And I realize, "Wait a minute. That guide, who went before me, is bigger than me and weighs more than I do. And he didn't die. So maybe I won't die."

So I take a deep breath and take that one step into infinity...

And *Wheeeeeee!*

I have the time of my life!

It's so fun, so exhilarating, I can't wait to do it again!

Today, I actually *lead* zip lining adventures with my DREAM Mastermind clients (that's where I work with entrepreneurs for a year to help them build their business to 6- and 7-figure levels).

And every time, I have a blast!

The point of the story is this: Sometimes our brains will tell us things that aren't true.

Your brain's job is to keep you safe. But sometimes "playing it safe" is the most dangerous thing you can do.

Not only will you miss out on life, you won't allow yourself to grow and experience the best that life has to offer.

Next time you're "on the platform" faced with a

choice like I had, you basically have those same 3 choices: back down and go backwards; stay where you are; or go forward.

The funny thing about life, though, is that life doesn't really allow us to go backward or stay in place. That's why the only realistic choice is to go forward.

And once you do it, I'll bet you find it's not as scary as you thought it would be.

Oh, and one more thing...

When you're thinking of trying something new, it's helpful to know that other people have tried it before you, and they didn't die. In fact, not only did they <u>not</u> die, they actually changed their lives for the better.

Bottom line: Sometimes it just takes one step of faith to change your life!

How I Discovered Afformations®

In April 1997, I was a struggling religious studies major in college. I had been reading self-help books for years but I was still a failure. I was broke, unhappy and lonely. Most of all, I felt very frustrated.

At the time, I was living in a tiny college dorm room that was so small, if you stood in the middle of the room and put your arms out to the side, you could touch the walls on both sides! And I had all of my worldly possessions in this tiny little room.

So I kept thinking to myself, *"What am I missing? What am I doing wrong? And how can I get out of this lousy situation?"*

One night in 1997, as I was sitting alone in my tiny dorm room, I happened to notice all of these little pieces of paper on the walls of my room. On these little pieces of yellow paper were positive affirmations that I'd written. Statements like: *I am happy, I am rich, I am healthy, I am wealthy and I am successful.*

Why had I written all those positive statements and put them on my walls? Because every self-help book I'd read had TOLD me to do that! The problem was, they weren't working for me at all.

In fact, I felt even *more* frustrated, because I thought, "How come I'm doing exactly what they told me to do – and it's STILL not working??"

I went to bed that night feeling more frustrated than ever.

The Shower That Changed Everything

The next morning, I got in the shower like any other morning. But on this particular morning, my head was still spinning, thinking about these questions. Thoughts kept rattling around my head, like: "If you want to change your life, you have to change your beliefs. But what is a belief?"

Then I realized, a belief is a thought.

So I asked myself, "What is thought?"

The more I thought about it, I realized that *human thought* is *the process of asking and searching for answers to questions.*

For example, if I were to ask you, *why is the sky blue?*

What happens in your brain?

Your brain starts to *search for the answer to the question.*

So I said to myself, "If the human mind is automatically searching for answers to questions, why are we going around making *statements that we don't believe?"*

The Cure for the Common Statement

We all know that affirmations are statements of something that you want to be true.

For example, a classic affirmation is: *I am rich.*

Now, say that statement to yourself: "I am rich."

What does your brain say?

Your brain is probably saying, *"Yeah, right!"*

Because you really don't believe the statement you're saying.

But we've been taught to say these positive statements over and over again, which essentially means we've been told to "pound our brains into submission."

So as I was standing there in the shower all those years ago, I had a thought... a thought that would change my life... and change the lives of hundreds of thousands of people around the world.

My thought was, "What if there was a simpler, faster, easier way to change our beliefs and change our lives? What if, instead of saying statements we don't believe, we simply started to *ask better questions?*"

For example, you say *I am rich* and your brain says, *Yeah, right!*

What, then, would the question be?

Why am I so rich?

When you ask that question, what immediately happens in your brain?

Exactly...

You start to *search for the answer to the question.*

As You Sow, So Shall You Reap

We've all heard the ancient law: *As you sow, so shall you reap.*

What are we really sowing? We're sowing *seeds of thought.*

But what are most people doing? *They are*

sowing lousy thought seeds.

Seeds like, *why am I so broke? Why am I so fat? How come my business isn't growing? Why is there more <u>month</u> left at the end of the <u>money</u>?*

When you ask lousy questions, what do you get?

Exactly! Lousy answers.

And lousy answers lead to a lousy life.

So I thought: "What if, instead of asking lousy questions and getting lousy answers and creating a lousy life... what if we flipped the whole thing on its head... started *asking empowering questions* that lead to *phenomenal answers* and create a *wonderful life?*"

And that's why, as I was standing in the shower on April 24, 1997, I said to myself, "Holy cow! I think I just invented something!"

So I had to give it a name... and the name I gave it was **Afformations®.**

Since then, **Afformations -** <u>not</u> "affirmations" – have been called "the missing piece to a life of abundance and prosperity" by many of the world's leading experts, as well as thousands of my clients and students around the world.

And for many, it represents "the missing piece" that everyone has been looking for...

My "4A Method" to Change Your Life with

Afformations®

Step 1: ASK yourself what you want.

You can use a goal you've previously written down, or start from scratch. You decide.

(Please note that traditional success teachers stop right here. They tell you to "set your goals" and then say "affirmations" trying to convince your brain that you have what you want. How's that working for you?)

For example, Sheila, an entrepreneur from California, had spent over $30,000 on self-help programs with little to show for it. When she came to me, her sales averaged $5000 a month.

I encouraged her to follow this formula. For this step, Sheila wrote: *"I want to make more money in my business."*

Then I taught her the breakthrough step...

Step 2: AFFORM an empowering question that assumes that what you want is <u>already true</u>.

In Sheila's example, I taught her to ask WHY she was making more money in her business. So her **Afformation** was: *"Why did I make more money so quickly and easily?"*

You can afform about anything you want – to attract more clients, get your book published, find love, overcome addiction, lose weight, and more.

(And yes, my clients have manifested all of these things... and more!)

Step 3: ACCEPT the truth of your new question.

The point of **Afformations** does not lie in finding "the answer", but in asking better questions. When you ask better questions, your mind will start to focus on things you've probably never thought about before. When you do this, the results will amaze you.

For example, you can read, write, speak, and listen to your new **Afformations.** It only takes a few minutes a day to change your beliefs and change your life.

Step 4: ACT based on your new assumptions.

We all make assumptions based on our beliefs. But using Afformations, you can make conscious and clear that which has, until now, been subconscious and hidden.

For example, after Sheila followed the first 3 steps, she then started doing things a top money earner would do. She hired an assistant. She hired a mentor (me). She started taking new actions based on her new assumptions.

One year later, Sheila's sales had grown from $5000 per month to ***over $75,000 per month.***

Afformations aren't magic, they're science. Thousands of people have experienced incredible breakthroughs with **Afformations**, from doubling their income to losing weight to finding the love of their lives.

To learn more about *Afformations*®, get *The Book of Afformations*® at www.noahsnewbook.com and my Afformations® Mastery Formula at www.havingabundance.com

Noah St. John is a keynote speaker and best-selling author who is famous for inventing Afformations® and helping busy executives and mission-driven entrepreneurs boost income and enjoy financial freedom.

His sought-after advice is known as the "secret sauce" in personal and business growth.

Noah's dynamic and down-to-earth speaking style always gets high marks from audiences. As the leading authority on how to eliminate limiting beliefs, Noah delivers live programs and online courses that have been called **"the only training that FIXES every other training!"**

He also appears frequently in the news worldwide, including ABC, NBC, CBS, Fox, The Hallmark Channel, National Public Radio, *Parade, Woman's Day, Los Angeles Business Journal, The Washington Post, Chicago Sun-Times, Selling Power, Forbes.com,* and *The Huffington Post.*

Get Noah's new book ***Mastering the Inner Game of Success*** FREE at **www.NoahStJohn.com**

"Focus first and results follow."
~ Michael Jenkins

Develop a Winning Culture Through Leadership

Align with Your Values and Passion

Rebecca Herman, PhD

Successful leaders are champions of culture.

I was that annoying kid who always asked "why" to everything. As I grew up, developed relationships, and worked in a variety of industries, that nature of "why" stayed with me. It was as if I had to know "why." That need seemed to push aside any shyness or potential anxiety so that I could walk right up to a person and ask them about their organization.

Eventually, the answers started to have a familiar ring: people. It's all about people; who they are, how they fit in the organization, shared values, working together and forming meaningful relationships. It started to become obvious that organizations are living things because without the people, they are just brick and mortar.

The people connection led to a desire to learn how organizations truly work and what makes one successful when another seemingly similar organization fails. I'm not sure when it happened but my epiphany was the realization that what I had learned and experienced was truly organizational culture. It had permeated my life and interests since before I could define it.

I now understand that successful leaders recognize that organizational culture is their responsibility and know how to use it effectively. They are champions of culture. It can be challenging because culture depends on the beliefs and attitudes of all of the organization's members. These shared beliefs drive behavior. The pooled behavior of the individual members creates cultural norms such as habits, values, and customs. Culture is a collective behavior; thus, not duplicatable. Think about that for a moment. Not duplicatable. How many strategies can make this claim? When leaders focus on culture, they can create and maintain a true competitive advantage.

To bring this to life, I will share three different examples of organizational culture in action. The first is about being truly committed to values. The second concerns the danger of not hiring for cultural fit. The final example demonstrates how passion can ignite a truly winning culture.

The Importance of Commitment to Values

After eight years in retail store management, I was ready for a change. TJ Maxx was opening a 1.2 million square foot distribution center in Evansville, IN and I was selected to be part of the start-up team as an on-site merchant. Before I knew it, I was driving to Worcester, MA where I would live and be immersed in training for six months. Our training was split between learning distribution operations, merchandise allocation and side-by-side work in New York City with our assigned buyers.

The true challenge of learning was not in what was being taught but in the need to navigate fluctuating cultural norms with each assignment. The distribution leadership team did not seem committed to the company values of being integrity driven, caring, and focused on people development. They also made it clear they did not want us training in their facility or learning the fine details of how goals were achieved.

My frustration came to a head and I wrote a heart-felt letter to Ben Cammarata, Founder and CEO of TJ Maxx, concerning the leadership team's lack of commitment to the corporate values. I was stunned, and concerned, to receive a call from his office inviting me to a private meeting. I spent two hours in Ben's office discussing concerns and observations... then just listening to him, his vision and his hopes. Looking back I realize how incredible this really was!

Changes were made based on our conversation as a tipping point. Ben believed in the culture he was building and wanted to ensure that everyone in a leadership role was on board with that as well. Throughout my tenure with the organization, Ben or one of his top VPs would check in with me each year to see how things were going. I will never forget his commitment to people and living the values that he held dear.

The Danger of Not Hiring for Cultural Fit

In 1997, I joined the Maintenance Warehouse, a Home Depot subsidiary. Shortly thereafter, Bernie Marcus and Arthur Blank, Founders, visited our San Diego offices as they were very active in all aspects of the business. They led by example by always demonstrating how our actions should reflect the values of respect, customer service and giving back.

Three years later, the Bernie and Arthur retired and Bob Nardelli took the helm. He brought the GE culture of hard-hitting performance and expectations of extreme efficiency to the organization. This may have worked well in a manufacturing environment but was not aligned for a customer-focused industry like ours. Store sales plummeted, employee morale sunk, and the changing culture affected all aspects of the business.

Although Nardelli achieved short-term gains from efficiency, it cost the organization its most valuable assets, its people – both employees and customers. He assumed that what worked at one organization would work equally as well at another. He did not look at the cultural differences or what type of culture was truly needed to be successful in this particular industry, what had made The Home Depot a true retail giant. Values were misaligned with his strategy. The Home Depot and Nardelli mutually agreed to part ways after six years but the damage had been done.

Allow Passion to Ignite a Winning Culture

As a huge baseball fan, it was an honor to co-author a book on the leadership in Major League Baseball. That journey included spending the day with many teams and the opportunity for an in-depth interview with managers about leadership. In 2012, Ned Yost was the manager of the Kansas City Royals - a team with typically pretty low expectations regarding the playoffs. My interview with Yost provided insight as to how he was changing the culture and expectations of his team.

When asked who had the greatest influence on his career, Yost noted that there were three people that he attributed his success. First, Bobbie Cox, he coached under him with the Atlanta Braves for twelve years and they went to the playoffs each year. Under Cox he was able to watch how he treated people and what strong relationships meant to developing a winning team. Next was former teammate, Ted Simmons. Ned said that Teddy taught him how to truly study the game. This brought in the strategy side of baseball from a player's perspective.

Finally, he said that Dale Earnhardt, the racecar driver, taught him how to compete. They were best friends. Dale knew how to win championships and truly wanted the same for his friend. Dale had hoped Ned would be at his side to celebrate another Daytona 500 victory but the Braves had a Spring Training game. There was no NASCAR victory on that day - Dale lost his life on the track during the final lap. Ned keeps an empty champagne bottle in his office from a previous Daytona celebration to remind him of the passion to compete. He also now wears the number 3 on his uniform (Earnhardt's car number) to keep his friend with him during games.

I felt that the Royals were on the verge of enormous success and I shared my feelings with Yost. Two years later he took that team to the

Rebecca Herman

World Series and it came down to the final game (#7) for the Giants to finally win the championship. Regardless, the Royals had gone farther than any KC team had in decades and their winning culture would be in the history books. I believe they have a championship in their future.

Tips for Creating Your Winning Culture

Here are five tips to start using organizational culture as a competitive advantage.

Tip 1 - Conduct a Culture Audit

The first step is to conduct a culture audit so you truly know where you stand. Even if you believe you have a good culture, going through an audit process will be very enlightening, as it will identify strengths and opportunities for improvement. It is important to remember that this must be driven from top leadership with both a willingness to take action and the ability to implement desired modifications on the identified gaps. While implementation can be accomplished in-house, there are many benefits to bringing in an outside consultant to identify existing values and behaviors, check for alignment and diagnose barriers to achieving stated goals.

185

Tip 2 - Clarify Values

With the culture audit completed, it is an opportune time to clarify your organization's core values. These are the guiding principles that direct behavior and action for members of the organization. Again, this is work for the senior leadership team and it is often helpful to have an outside consultant provide objective facilitation of the process. You will discuss the existing practiced values from the culture audit and brainstorm about values that are important to achieve your vision. In order to operationalize the values, be certain to discuss examples of decisions that would be made with the values in mind. Identify behaviors that support each of the core values and determine how those behaviors will be measured.

Tip 3 - Align Strategy and Culture

This is a critical step that too many leaders overlook and then cannot understand why they are unable to achieve their stated strategy. Many leaders desire to bring high levels of innovation into their organization; however, they may still have the behaviors of a former strategy, such as quality. Innovation requires risk taking, action and a wide array of thoughts. This is quite different from the discipline, best practices and process improvement required to achieve quality. You may have discovered there are gaps in your culture from the audit. If so, address them before attempting a new strategic direction.

Tip 4 - Hire for Fit

Too often we spend our time crafting job descriptions that include a long list of knowledge, skills and abilities. Yes, you may hire a brilliant person with amazing experience but they still may not last due to not fitting the culture. Even Major League Baseball teams suffer from this; they sign many All-Star players in the off-season with the hope of winning a championship only to discover that they don't play as a team. Use behavior-based interviewing to discover how a candidate fits with the organization's values, belief and work style. Remember that you can train someone on company-specific skills but it is nearly impossible to change their values and beliefs.

Tip 5 - Reward the Right Behaviors

At this point, you have identified the culture and strategy that will help you achieve your goals and have hired the people to get you there. This step brings it all together. Performance management is truly about reinforcing the behaviors we want to see in the organization. This is the HOW THINGS GET DONE component.

Systems should be developed that measure goals not only for *what* is accomplished but also *how* it is accomplished. It should be simple enough for clear communication across the organization. Don't forget to take time to celebrate, reward and recognize regularly!

It is in Your Hands

At our core, we want to succeed; to be number one; earn the spotlight and accolades of our peers. This may include being recognized in our community or in our industry. Perhaps your organization aspires to receive national recognition such as the *Malcolm Baldrige National Quality Award* or *Fortune's 100 Best Companies to Work For*. In Major League Baseball, we may start the season saying we want to win your division but in reality, every team and every player truly wants to win the World Series Championship. And why not? Maybe this is our year! But we must have vision and the passion to execute the plan to achieve our greatest dreams. And before we can do that - we must ask - is the culture of my organization our greatest asset? It should be. It can be. Make it happen.

Rebecca Herman, PhD, has been passionate about organizational culture for nearly 30 years. She learned early in her career that it is truly the people of the organization, their beliefs and behaviors that drive results. Rebecca loves to help leaders identify the culture that they need in order to truly enact their core values and achieve their optimum strategy for success.

Rebecca's ability to look at each situation with fresh eyes and an open mind brings enormous value to her clients. With two decades in Human Resources, a decade in Higher Education, and three decades in volunteer leadership for her sorority, Dr. Herman has a wide range of experiences and practical knowledge in organizational culture and leadership. Whether speaking professionally or serving as a leadership consultant, Rebecca will help you achieve a Winning Culture!

Please visit Dr. Herman's website where you may download a **FREE** guidebook: 7 ways to Develop a Winning Culture!

Email: Rebecca@WinningCultureLeadership.com
Website: www.WinningCultureLeadership.com

Be What You Want To Be, Or Not To Be

Don-Alan Rekow

Most people spend all their lives being what someone else wants them to be. It takes a clear vision, resolute tenacity, constant focus, a healthy confidence and a lot of guts to be what you want to be.

Back in 1999, I worked for Hog Building Systems (HBS), a company in Spain that built turn-key hog breeding operations. I began as a welder and rapidly progressed my way up through the company. Within 6 months I was asked to manage a project being built for 2500 sows. When that finished a year later I was asked to work in the engineering department at the home office in Barcelona. While in that department I also became the field resource for our American supplier, working with their engineers to help them solve any problems we had with the equipment.

My wide array of experience allowed me to excel in any position that I was put into. The engineers themselves, the ones with the titles and schooling, often came to me to ask what I thought of different problems they had encountered; mostly because I knew what would work and what wouldn't. Rather than learning theory in a classroom, experience was my teacher. Late one afternoon I arrived at the office where two engineers, the CAD operator, the owner and the product salesman were all trying to figure out a problem. They asked for my advice and instantly I told them how it could be fixed. My response was NOT what they wanted to hear, so the debate began, me against them. *They* wanted me to tell *them* how to make *their* idea work, instead of accepting the solution I gave. After about 2 hours, several phone calls and a lot of reasoning, they finally understood why their idea would not work and they accepted the course of action I had given in the beginning as the solution to the problem. It was not that I wanted to be right; I simply understood the problem and what needed to be done to correct it. The proper course of correction would take longer than they wanted, so they were seeking an easy way out. I had previously faced a similar problem, so I had already learned what needed to be done. There was no need to theorize the solution; I already had the solution.

Life itself and the "School of Hard Knocks" have been my teachers. I have not always been the best student, as I have had to repeat courses. Wisdom is defined in the dictionary as: *the quality or state of being wise; knowledge of what is true or right, coupled with judgment as to what to put into action; sagacity, discernment, or insight.* However, at times, our judgment is clouded with our own reasons for wanting to be right or for things to be done our own way.

Being wise, having the power of discerning, and judging properly as to what is true or right— possessing discernment, judgment, or discretion is a very valuable asset to possess. *Wisdom* is void of personal preferences or needs; it is key to success in anything. It is imperative to be able to separate your own feelings and need to be right from what is true or right. There is not nearly enough space here to thoroughly cover this topic. I have however, already written over 1000 pages and recorded many hours of video about this subject which I teach in a model called COnCEPT Q.[1]

As we get older and wiser we tend to seek the advice of individuals who are more mature and seasoned with experienced on the topic we want to learn. This is the wise thing to do. That is what

---

[1] COnCEPT Q is written about by Don-Alan Rekow in *There Is No Personal Power in Chaos,* touted as "one of the finest personal development books ever written." To get this idea in print was the original reason he went into the publishing business.

this *Experts Wisdom* book is all about.

In the year 2000, when a down turn in the porcine market hit Europe, HBS chose me to be the first of their downsizing since I was one of their higher paid employees. I was ok with the loss of the job; it allowed me to do what I had always wanted to do; become a published author.

I had already written my first book, had taken it to several publishers and was turned down by all of them. I decided that I would have to publish it myself. So from ready-to-be-published author, I became the publisher. This thought was a very dangerous one, as it led me down a very expensive and time consuming path. Having already been in business for myself several times before, this time I wanted to do everything right and I did my due diligence to insure my success. I enrolled in a six month business course which taught me how to put my business together. I also learned additional skills that were applicable to my new venture of becoming a publisher and took a comprehensive computer class to be sure I had all the training I needed to get started.

During my business class, I identified that there was no bindery in the province where we lived. I decided that in addition to the publishing company, we could also provide post-press services to the local print shops which would also fund my publishing company. That's where I realized my big mistake. I was side tracked from my goal of becoming a published author by starting down the path of becoming the publisher and then became even more distracted by the possibility of being the bindery as well, which in hindsight, is a path that I did *not* want to trod.

Do what you really want to do, not something else you think may be related to it.

I was told by someone in the bindery business that if he had it to do all over again, he would invest in a beach property and forget the bindery. I chose to ignore the underlying warning that came with that statement thinking that he did not understand my intentions. Years later, I wish I would have listened to him in that moment. For me, trying to put together a bindery was just adding a lot of unnecessary work and expense to my original objective. It was something related to what I really wanted to do, but not my heart's true desire.

Choose your path as an author or take the detour as a publisher? That is the question.

Think back to when you decided that you wanted to write your book. Review all the effort it took to get it to the ready-to-publish stage. If you are a do-it-yourselfer, what do you think would be the next logical stage? Become the publisher, correct? Let's talk about becoming the publisher for just a moment.

Back in 2000 when I was making the decision to become a publisher, Print-on-Demand (POD) was just beginning and was really a novel idea in Spain. My intention was to become a publisher and put together a POD shop, but I was persuaded to do much more for the local post-press market. In many ways, this was a costly decision. Over the next 13 years our business had ups and downs with all kinds of start-up pains and was finally transformed into the publishing company that I originally envisioned. When my wife and I finally decided to move back to the US at the end of 2013, the decision to establish the company in the US was greatly influenced by the types of publishing companies that already existed. The *traditional publishing company* and the *self-publishing publisher* which assisted the author were the main two models. There was another kind known as the *vanity press* which was the pay-to-get-your-book-in-print model where some larger printers would print your book for you without the use of a publisher. Our form of publishing leaned heavily toward the POD self-publishing model because my brother already had a POD printing company set up. The key that stood out to me as the bridge from the self-publishing to the traditional model was mainly offering services to help the author build his or her own platform.

The traditional publisher is not interested in building the platform for a new author. They want the author to come to the table with their platform already established. If a traditional method publisher is willing to make an investment in the author, the author must prove promising in order to elicit the investment. The author becomes "captive" to the publisher as well.

The self-publishing model offers different packages, however in a smorgasbord fashion to be added to the basic package. Every option costs additional money. At SAbER Mountain our objective was to combine both worlds and create a hybrid publisher.

What makes SAbER Mountain different from other hybrid publishers is that we build complete platforms for our authors with a limited investment on their part, maximizing the highest royalties and offering low cost printing.

We also:

- build websites
- film video
- create product
- record audio
- build crowd funding platforms to raise money for the project.

Our objective is to help our authors with pieces of their platforms they do not have.

Stick to your original objective as an author.

If your true objective is to become an author to further validate your own expertise and business idea with a book, it is most logical that you would build a platform to promote you, your book and your business rather than head off onto some other trail like that of becoming the publisher.

Allow me to share with you several steps to successfully add the title of *Author* to your list of accomplishments and accolades that will enhance *your* expertise.

Complete Your Manuscript

Many people want to write a book and only have the idea, but not the manuscript for the book. There are several ways to get your book written, but the best is to just sit down and do it. At SAbER Mountain we have book coaches who can help, knowing that is a hard task to accomplish. Make sure that it is complete with all the references and support material needed. Don't try to format the book. Too many people want to "see" what the book is going to look like and use a word processor to prepare the book for print. Resist that temptation! Lay it out as double-spaced text without trying to format it. Books have to be laid out in a design program, and if you take it to a printer in a format that they do not want, it could be returned and they definitely will not want to fix it for you. Files must be press-ready and I can state that most people do not know what the printer needs.

Select a Publisher

If you are a first time author, decide what route you would like to take. Please understand that you probably will not get selected by a traditional publisher on your first book. Of all the manuscripts sent to them, only about three percent are chosen, and many of those are repeat authors or very well-known people. Let your publisher provide the ISBN for you. A single ISBN is expensive, and was made that way to discourage individuals from getting just one ISBN. Let your publisher do that work for you.

Build Your Platform

In addition being asked about how to become a published author, I am most frequently asked how to become a *best-selling* author. The answer is... *build your platform*! What kind of reach do you already have? What are you doing to extend that reach? What do you offer your public? This is the real key to having a best-selling book, not just becoming an author.

Don't spend all your life being what someone else wants you to be. Let becoming an author enhance you and your expertise. Focus on what is important to you and remember; *do what you really want to do. Allowing other objectives to take you off course will only delay your original desire.*

If you could watch a movie where you knew the outcome and the result was the success of your objectives... how would you act today?

Don-Alan Rekow is the author of *There Is No Personal Power in Chaos* which has been acclaimed as "one of the finest personal development books ever written." He is the creator of the COnCEPT Q system described in the book. He founded SAbER Mountain Publishers and iSAbER TV to further teach the concept.

After living in Spain for 21 years, his recent return to the US allows him to focus on building *SAbER Integrated Publishing Platform* (SIPP) for new and upcoming authors. This hybrid model of publishing is designed to help authors target and sell to their markets without consistently having to spend a fortune.

As an entrepreneur from early youth, one of Don's passions is to help youth understand business and to consider the importance of building their own businesses as a viable means to rebuild the greatness of America, teaching them how to fish rather than handing them a fish. Learn more at www.Don-AlanRekow.com.

Success, Goosebumps & Your Next Evolution

Barbara Niven

*Live your passion. Connect to your purpose.
Make a difference. And don't give up five
minutes before the miracle.*

Do you ever have a nagging feeling that there's more to life than what you're living? If so, there probably is. Stop deflecting the message and listen to it. Don't settle for just "okay" if you know there's something more you are here to do. Instead, use it as a new starting point to reach even higher.

Our dreams change as we evolve. It's important to revisit them often to create new goals and strategies. If the rush is gone, go find it again! Recommit to an old dream or find a new one! Kick it up a notch and break out of your old routine. Do you need to revise or reinvent anything in yourself or your surroundings? Well, then do it! Shake it up. Don't play safe.

Fall in love again with your possibilities.

Surround yourself with people who make things happen. Re-inspire yourself through the work of Artists, thought leaders and revolutionary thinkers. Let their passion reignite yours. Get so hungry you can taste it! Then take action.

Decide what you want your Life Legacy to be. When all is said and done, what do you want people to say about you? What do you want to be remembered for? Will your time here on earth have made a difference?

Life is short, and there are no guarantees. Stop squandering energy on things that don't matter. If you knew you only had a year, or six months, or even tomorrow to live... how would you spend your time? Would your priorities change? Why wait? Change them now.

You have greatness within you, and you are here for a Purpose. But sometimes it's hard to connect the dots because we overthink it. We often say to ourselves, "Who am I to do big things?" Well, who are you not to! As Marianne Williamson said, playing small doesn't serve the world!

Not sure where to begin? Here's a great place to start, and it's simple. What gives you joy? What would you pay someone to let you do? What gives you goosebumps and makes you smile at the sheer audaciousness of it? THAT'S IT.

The secret is to FOLLOW YOUR GOOSEBUMPS.

Tap into that power and potential, kick yourself into gear and start playing full out. Notice I said the word "play?" Living your passion is truly the most fun thing in the world and will GPS you right smack into your purpose.

If you're like most people, as we get older we start to edit ourselves. Throw that out the window for a moment. Take all the negativity out of the equation and simply ask yourself, "What would I do if I knew I could not fail?"

Allow that to sink in. What WOULD you do? What COULD you do?!! Are you smiling at the possibilities? What's stopping you? The only thing you know for sure is that if you never start, failure is a certainty.

Remember back to when you were a little kid with big dreams and a big imagination. When you believed that anything and everything were possible! Are you still living full out like that? If not, maybe you've forgotten who you really are.

Life has a way of erasing us down into something small and careful and "less than." Think back to when you saw possibilities instead of obstacles, giggled uncontrollably at silly things, and flew as high as you could go on a swing simply trying to touch the sky.

Reconnect with that courageous, spunky, irrepressible little kid you used to be. Hug her, thank her and applaud her. She is still there inside, jumping at the chance to play with you again. Isn't it time to let her out and let her lead for a change?

My acting dream scared the heck out of me. But I remember thinking, "20 years from now I don't want to wonder 'what if?' I need to know if I can make it as an actress!" What a gift I gave myself then. I would have ended up this age anyway – dream or not! I am grateful that I decided to take the leap when I did.

That's not the only dream that has frightened me. I've constantly reinvented myself over the years, and each time I've had to push through scary personal barriers. One of the biggest was when I decided to become an entrepreneur and create my *Unleash Your Star Power!* media training business and video studio.

Talk about being out of my comfort zone! Yes, I was absolutely comfortable in front of the camera, but behind it? ACKK! I had to rent and furnish a studio, study lighting techniques, buy and use camera equipment, learn video editing, create a home study course, develop an online academy, write books, find business coaches, etc. - plus go out and sell myself and my business by speaking on stages! What a journey. It's been a leap of faith all the way.

I remember when my very first client, a CEO, was flying in to work with me. I had rented a very tiny room for my first studio, and as he was in the cab from the airport my friend was showing me which buttons to push on the camera. I was sweating bullets, but it worked out great and I was able to really help him get over his public speaking fears. He said it was life-changing. That's still my favorite part about working with clients. I get goosebumps helping them hone their message, step into their power and transform as I shoot their videos!

Today, six years later, I have an amazing professional studio and my business has grown to where I am proud to be known as Hollywood's Top Media Trainer and Video Marketing Coach. Sometimes I still pinch myself. Did I really do that?!!

"If I never try, I'll never know" is a phrase that has fueled and pushed me through great leaps in my life. Most of the times, thank goodness, I have landed on my feet; or at least learned a valuable lesson that served me well later.

Another lesson I have learned is to always say "YES!" and then figure out the details later. I would have missed so much otherwise, especially in the entertainment industry, which moves at lightning speed. For example... three years ago I was in Phoenix just getting ready to go on stage to speak for an audience of 200 people, when I got a call from my manager that Hallmark Channel wanted me to do a new TV series, *"Cedar Cove."* He said they were offering me the part, but that I'd have to be on a plane to Vancouver in two days! I had no idea how I was going to make it work because I wasn't even in the same state to pack! But I said "YES!" and trusted that it would work out. It did. What a blessing it's been! We just finished shooting our third season of *"Cedar Cove"* and I'm proud to say that I'm now also doing a second series, *"Murder She Baked"* for Hallmark Movies and Mysteries.

When was the last time you said YES to something that scared you? If it's been awhile, you're playing too safe. Today, try something different. If your first inclination is always NO, pause before it pops out of your mouth. Say "yes" and see what happens. Get out of your comfort zone. Only with great risk, comes great reward.

Fear and excitement both manifest the same way. They both create butterflies in the stomach, sweaty palms, heart palpitations—and goosebumps! Embrace them, steady yourself and then LEAP, even if you can't see a net underneath you, because everything you ever wanted may be waiting on the other side!

I hope you choose to leap every chance you get too. That first jump off the cliff is the hardest and it may be a wild and bumpy ride as you find your wings. But it is the only way you'll ever see how high you can fly. It's worth the risk. And wow, talk about exhilaration!

Are you feeling a bit of trepidation here? Good. It means you're getting out of your comfort zone. And that's where the magic will happen!

My Big Dream began when I was a little girl. I always **knew** that I was going to be an actress, and I've always loved a camera. My family tells me that when we went on outings, like to the beach, I would disappear and they would find me down the beach posing and waving in front of some stranger's camera. There must be a lot of people who said, "Who is the chubby little blonde girl?" when they got their photos back.

At 21 years old, I was still waiting for my dream to happen. I actually remember thinking someone would come and "discover" me in Portland, Oregon. I still didn't understand that manifesting my dream would be up to me. It was so far out of my comfort zone that it didn't even occur to me! As I look back, I wish I could whisper to my younger self: "GO! Take the leap! Follow your Dreams! You will be just fine... and you will have the adventure of a lifetime!"

I let almost another decade go by before I finally took action. I put my dream on hold as I began to live everybody else's vision of what my life should be. I quit college after less than a year, got a job, got married, had a baby and started a business with my husband. Still, I always thought that "someday I'll do my acting dream."

One day an application for our ten-year high school reunion arrived in the mail. I couldn't believe that ten years had gone by! The form asked: *who did you marry, how many kids did you have*, and so on. The final question was, *Have you achieved all you thought you would in your life by now?*

I literally staggered. It hit me like a ton of bricks that I hadn't even *started* acting yet! It was a huge Aha moment and lesson. I realized that I alone am responsible for what I will – or will not – accomplish in my lifetime. From that moment on, I began thinking like the CEO of my life and career.

The first thing I did was consider my options. I hadn't finished college, and by now I was a single mother of a 2 year-old. But I thought, "I can write and I'm great in front of the camera. Why don't I become a TV reporter?"

Everybody told me it couldn't be done, but that always makes my fight kick in. I found two mentors. One was the news director at KGW, the NBC affiliate in Portland, and the other was a producer at PM Magazine. "If I bring you stories," I asked them, "Will you mentor me? Because I *am* going to work for you." They both took me on as an intern.

Here's where I first used my system, *ACT AS IF*! It means to *act as if it's already happening, until it is*. It's also called "assume the position." I would call a place, gather all my courage and all of my acting ability into my words and say, "Hi, I'm an associate producer with KGW. If I come in and pre-interview you, we may do a story on you. But I need to pre-produce you first." Of course, everyone wanted to be on TV. So I would interview my subject and then race home and write up the interview into a script, adding whatever video shots I imagined I would use if I had a real camera shooting it. The next day I'd go back, knock on their doors again and present my stories to my mentors. They were shocked to see me back so soon! But they liked my moxie, and I was good at it. And I was persistent. Finally KGW hired me as an intern and I sold my very first story to network.

Then I heard that ABC Daytime casting was on a nationwide tour, searching for an actress to replace Tina on *"One Life to Live."* They were making a stop in Seattle. It didn't matter that I'd never taken an acting class; I just knew I had to go. So I went to a bookstore and picked out a monologue from Neil Simon's *"Chapter Two."* I didn't perform it for anyone—I practiced it silently, over and over, in my head. I loved the process. I could really relate to my character and I poured my heart and soul into it.

When the day of the audition came, a winter

black ice storm raged outside and it shut down the whole Pacific Northwest, including the airports. I, however, had waited long enough to put my dream into action. So I bundled up, hopped in my car, and drove from Portland to Seattle for the casting call. Nobody else was on the road because it was sheer ice.

When I got there I changed in the car, fixed my makeup and went in. They taped my audition and ten minutes later I was back in my car, heading home, completely transformed and empowered by the experience. Unbelievably, the next week ABC flew me out to New York for a screen test! That's when I knew I was on the right track. I didn't get the part that time, but ironically, I was on the series twenty years later!

After that audition, I knew exactly what I wanted. I had plugged into my passion and I was "home." People thought I was crazy to risk everything for such an intangible career! But I did it anyway because the thought of not at least *trying* was worse.

I eventually packed up a U-Haul, installed my little daughter as copilot and moved us to L.A. It was a real struggle and at times we were so poor. But we have had an extraordinary life, full of love and support for each other's dreams. My daughter says that it was the best gift I ever gave her, teaching her that the secret to life is doing what you love and figuring out how to make a living at it.

Every moment is a fresh start... a new chance to go toward your dream or away from it. What's so great is that even after a major backslide, you can change it all in the next second. NOT taking action is also a choice. Too many people allow those single moments turn into years as time and opportunities slip away.

If you've recently make a bad choice somewhere, or are regretting missed opportunities, quit beating yourself up. It's done. It was only a blip on the radar. Don't dwell on it. Move on. Hook back into your dream and leap into the next moment! You'll be back on track stronger than ever, armed with a fresh perspective and new lessons learned.

Mine has been an incredible journey, with huge ups and downs and life lessons, but they've only made me stronger. Each time I hit a wall I was forced to take stock, change and grow to the next level.

Don't wonder "what if" someday. If you're ready for a change, take the drama out of it. Quit battling over the "whys and hows." You're making it harder than it needs to be. It's funny how we add drama, angst and stress to the equation, isn't it? Stop worrying, get over yourself and just do it. One, two, DONE and you can check it off your list.

Change doesn't happen all at once anyway. It's

a series of small actions, taken diligently, that will lead you to a different destination. If you don't like where it takes you, try something else. But keep moving. Like my wonderful, wise acting coach Milton Katselas used to say, *"You already know apple pie. Why not have a bite of cherry pie and see what you like better?"*

It is about Progress, not Perfection. Celebrate every small "win" along the journey. Even the losses have lessons, so learn to embrace them too.

Milton would also say, "The one who gets up from the mat the most times wins." I can't tell you how many times I've been down on that mat wondering how I'm going to get up again. But I always do, with a new resolve and fierceness to make it happen. That attitude has made all the difference in my career and my life.

It has become my passion and my mission to convince others that if I can live this crazy dream of being an actress, anybody can do anything - no matter who they are or where they come from.

Isn't it time to declare your passion for yourself and truly get on Purpose? I'll support you any way I can. In fact, I would love to personally invite you to join my Dreamers Network at

www.facebook.com/barbaraniven.

I have been blessed to be living this crazy acting dream! I've had amazing mentors, and started the Dreamers Network in 1998 as a way of paying it forward. I call it a "support group" for us Dreamers, because the world can be a very negative place. We must help each other and surround ourselves with people who lift us up, not put us down.

If you're a fellow Dreamer, I invite you to participate. Look around and you'll find amazing posts from people in all walks of life and corners of the globe. We flow advice and inspiration to each other, and would love to help support you too. Feel free to jump on in! Here's to your success as we go onward and upward together. As one succeeds, we all do. I'm proud to share this journey with you.

So... what's your passion? What would you most regret never doing? What's on your bucket list? Well, what are you waiting for?!! Go make this the year that changes everything!

Barbara Niven, award-winning actress, currently stars in the prime time TV series' *"Cedar Cove"* & *"Murder She Baked"* for Hallmark Channel, NBC's Emmy Award-winning "Parks and Recreation", *"Hamlet's Ghost"* which premiered at the Cannes Film Festival, and the independent comedy-horror feature *"Suburban Gothic."*

In addition to the 100+ Film and TV credits to her name, Barbara has gained international acclaim as Hollywood's Top Media Trainer and Video Marketing Coach. She created *Unleash Your Star Power!* to help others hone their message, makeover their professional image, handle nerves, and use video to dominate their niche. She works with new and established business owners, professionals, CEOs, entrepreneurs, hosts, speakers and authors from her studio in Los Angeles where she offers custom video production services, one-on-one coaching and her popular Video Boot Camps. Her new online academy is premiering soon.

She is also a Celebrity Motivational Speaker and best-selling author. Business and Motivational topics include *Unleash Your Star Power!, Be a Video Marketing Superstar, ACT as IF* and *Eating Disorders & Pressures to Be Perfect.* For more information, visit

www.UnleashYourStarPower.com.

-

Live your passion. Connect to your purpose.
Make a difference. And don't give up five minutes
before the miracle.
~ Barbara Niven

Becoming Unstoppable

Omar Periu

Success is in the moment,
make every moment count.

One of the things that I have found in becoming an expert in your field is to become unstoppable. Let me tell you my story...

I was born in Camaguey, Cuba into a very wealthy family and suddenly everything changed. Every fiber of my small, seven-year-old body was fearfully shaking as we walked through customs and explained the purpose of our trip: "We're vacationing in Miami," I heard my pregnant mother say as I clung to her dress. Even though I heard those words, I knew we would never be going home again.

Communism was quickly tightening the noose around the free enterprise system in Cuba, and my father, a successful entrepreneur, decided it was time to take his family and flee to a land where freedom, promise and opportunity thrived. Looking back now, it was the most courageous decision I've ever seen anybody make.

Castro's regime was watching my father very carefully, making it necessary for my mother to bring my brother and me over first. My father met us a few weeks later. Miami International Airport overwhelmed me. Everybody was speaking in strange words that didn't make sense to me. We had no money, no family - nothing but the clothes on our backs.

Within a few months, we were on a church-sponsored flight to Joliet, Illinois, via Chicago's O'Hare International Airport. A burst of cold air greeted us as we walked out of the terminal into the still talked about winter of 1961. It had snowed nearly four feet and amidst the blowing drifts stood a young priest by a large International Suburban, waiting to take us to our new home. This was absolutely amazing for a Cuban boy who had never seen snow.

My father was an educated man; he owned a chain of gas stations and a car dealership in Cuba. Unable to speak English, he adapted quickly by finding work as a mechanic; and thanks to St. Patrick's church, we were able to find a comfortable although small apartment in a middle-class neighborhood. We didn't have a lot, but we had one another, a whole lot of love and my father's burning desire to succeed.

It was during this tumultuous time that my

father, with his tattered Spanish copy of Dale Carnegie's book, *How to Win Friends and Influence People*, taught me one of the greatest lessons in life. He told me over and over again: *"It doesn't matter who you are, where you're from or what color you are. You can do anything you put your mind to."* These words gave me comfort, inspiration and hope; as my brother and I mixed into the great Chicago melting pot.

My brother Ed and I struggled in school because we couldn't speak English. Sadly, it wasn't uncommon to be called a "spic", to not to be chosen to be on a team or have our hand-me-down bikes stolen... but my father's words continued to burn inside of me... *"It doesn't matter who you are, where you're from or what color you are. You can do anything you put your mind to."* We ended up meeting some truly wonderful people who helped us overcome the obstacles of adjusting to our new surroundings. Many of these people are still my closest friends to this day.

When I was 14, my father was already teaching me about the great principle of free enterprise. He gave me $18 for every set of valves and engine heads I would clean and grind (what we called a valve job). Later he taught me how to hire other people to do the work for me, my first lessons in delegation and hiring. I later went out and found new customers and collected money – I basically ran the business. Little did I know he was teaching me how to be an entrepreneur. America was truly a land of promise!

I was fortunate to be born into a musically talented family and I remember listening to my mother singing beautiful Spanish songs to me as I was growing up. These songs inspired me to sing in the church choir as a boy soprano and because of this same influence, my brother Ed started a contemporary rock band. I attended every band rehearsal and at night harmonized with him and my mother. Later, through my earnings from working as a laborer in a stone quarry and with a scholarship, I studied opera and music at Southern Illinois University. After two years of college, I went back to work in the stone quarry and saved the money I earned for my move west to California.

My goal in moving to California was to break into the music business and cut my own records. It didn't take very long for reality to set in. I had to take a job selling health club memberships to support myself. Depression set in. I was broke and didn't know where to turn. Then I met Tom Murphy, one of the owners of the health club.

My father always told me that if you want to be wealthy, you have to do what wealthy people do, so I asked Mr. Murphy if we could talk over coffee to find out what made him so successful. It just so happened that Mr. Murphy was the business partner of Tom Hopkins, one of the country's top sales trainers. So, of course, he recommended that I start attending sales training seminars, reading self-improvement books and listening to sales tapes. He also introduced me to many successful business men and women and their published materials. I was so hungry for success that it didn't take long before I was the top salesperson in the company. But that wasn't good enough. After saving every penny I could, I invested in my own health club. By the time I was finished, I owned nine of the most successful health clubs and sports medicine facilities in the United States and by the age of 31, I was a multi-millionaire. We sold the clubs and he asked me to go on the road and teach others what he had taught me. So I decided to help others the way I was helped... to go from zero to wealth and drastically change peoples' lives. But I still hadn't achieved my goal to cut my own record.

Recording my first demo was exciting yet discouraging as I presented it to record company after record company. Each time I heard the word "no." Not to be defeated, I recorded the demo in Spanish and took it back to the same record companies, all with the same results. On the verge of giving up, I called my father to discuss what had happened. He said, "Omar, you're doing very well financially, aren't you?" I replied that I was. "Well, why don't you just buy a record company and record your music."

When I went back to the record company I intended to buy, hoping to save my ego, I asked the company executives one more time to record my music. They said, "Omar, we can't help you. Go to Broadway. You'll be great there." You should have seen their faces when I told them I was going to be the new owner.

I then set out to finance, record and produce my first album in Spanish. From there I went on to be named "Best Latin Male Vocalist" and Entertainer of the Year" in 1986, 1987, and 1988, "CHIN de PLATA" and "OTTO." One of the attributes of an expert is to be able to change careers and stay the unstoppable course. After achieving critical acclaim with my goal as a singer, I felt a void in my life; a need to help others. So I sat down with my mentor and decided to create a path for individuals, like myself, who were looking for more in their life. This took unstoppable reflections because I had to find what was to be my unique selling proposition. I had to find what would make my training materials and seminars special compared to others. After talks with my mentors, we found that my entrepreneur story of my struggles coming from Cuba could be a universal conversation for anyone that wanted to become an entrepreneur. That was my Expert Advisor Platform that we choose to add to my sales and management success.

What is your Expert Advisor Platform? Use the principals below to assist you in discovering your own platform.

Step One:
Set an outrageous goal statement; think bigger!

Step Two:
Create a mission Statement; Why do you want it? How will you benefit?

Step Three:
Analyze your position. Where are you starting from right now? More importantly, where do you want to go?

Step Four:
Identify the risks that you anticipate on your way to achieving this goal.

Step Five:
Identify the obstacles. List the obstacles that you anticipate on your way to achieving this goal.

Step Six:
Identify the investments and sacrifices. List the investments and sacrifices including time and money that you anticipate on your way to achieving this goal.

Step Seven:
Identify the additional knowledge that you will require to become the expert in your field.

Step Eight:
Identify the people whose help you will need; your influencers, coaches and mentors. What role will they play?

Step Nine:
Develop your plan. List everything you will have to do to achieve the goal. Prioritize your plan.

When you are looking to become an Expert Advisor you must first search for your specialty, what makes you shine and sets you apart from the rest. You must find a mentor who can help you begin the journey, continue and take you to completion successfully. It takes a mentor who's been through the process to guide you down the right path; which is one of the reasons why I began mentoring individuals and corporations myself. Because of my mentors, my openness to new ideas and ability to be coached I told myself "I will not be denied" and I became the success I am today!

I'm an entrepreneur with my own company, Omar Periu International; I have written multiple books, recorded CDs, DVDs and am involved with some of the largest motivational seminars in the world helping millions of people. I've been referred to as *"The #1 Motivational Teacher"* and have trained two thirds of the world's Fortune 500 Companies (over 4 million people) including... Oracle, Microsoft, Motorola, AT&T, Mercedes Benz, Lexus, Aflac and many, many more.

I'm a happily married father of two. My gorgeous wife Helen and I have been married for over two decades, with two beautiful children; Alexandra and Maxwell. My experiences and struggles as an immigrant have helped to shape my two children into the exceptional young people they are today. Due to my financial success I've been able to afford my children a superior education and expose them to other cultures which have brightened their horizons. It's such a thrill for me now to help others learn how to find the right opportunities to achieve their dreams and goals. Take it from me, my father was right: you can achieve anything you want in life when you set your mind to it.

To be the Unstoppable Expert Advisor, you must have a willingness to positively persist when others give you negativity.

I wish you great success!

Omar Periu proudly wears his rags to riches story for others to hear about and learn from. He went from making $147 a month at age 21 as a personal trainer to multi-millionaire status by age 31. He and his family fled Castro's regime when he was only 7; they arrived in Miami with no money, no family or friends in America and nothing but what they were wearing when they arrived.

Enduring many obstacles, Omar didn't let it embitter him. Instead, he made the most of his situation. His father, reading from a Spanish copy of "*How to Win Friends & Influence People*", taught Omar an important life lesson; "*It doesn't matter who you are, where you're from or what color you are, you can do anything you put your mind to."*

Omar has dedicated himself to helping others fulfill their dreams by teaching them how to achieve greatness! He specifically teaches how to set and achieve desired goals while ensuring constant and never ending improvement. More than a motivator, his peers refer to him as "*The Master Motivational Teacher.*"

www.OmarPeriu.com

Proof

Made in the USA
Charleston, SC
15 December 2015